HOPE AND THE
NEARNESS OF GOD

HOPE AND THE
NEARNESS OF GOD

The 2022 Lent Book

Teresa White FCJ

BLOOMSBURY CONTINUUM
LONDON · OXFORD · NEW YORK · NEW DELHI · SYDNEY

BLOOMSBURY CONTINUUM
Bloomsbury Publishing Plc
50 Bedford Square, London, WC1B 3DP, UK
29 Earlsfort Terrace, Dublin 2, Ireland

BLOOMSBURY, BLOOMSBURY CONTINUUM and the Diana logo
are trademarks of Bloomsbury Publishing Plc

First published in Great Britain 2021

A catalogue record for this book is available from the British Library

Library of Congress Cataloguing-in-Publication data has been applied for

ISBN: PB: 978-1-4729-8419-7; eBook: 978-1-4729-8420-3;
ePDF: 978-1-4729-8417-3

2 4 6 8 10 9 7 5 3 1

Typeset by Deanta Global Publishing Services, Chennai, India
Printed and bound in Great Britain by CPI Group (UK) Ltd, Croydon CR0 4YY

To find out more about our authors and books visit www.bloomsbury.com
and sign up for our newsletters

CONTENTS

INTRODUCTION

There are some words – and I do not think they are over-numerous – that belong to the vocabulary of the sacred. They include gentleness and kindness, love and joy. Generosity, patience and faithfulness would be among them too, as would peace. Most of these words are readily understood and are in common usage, but I think it is true to say that, in the rough and tumble of human discourse, they always have a special significance. When we say them, hear them, read them, reflect on them, they seem to draw us into the domain of God. Such words are in the truest sense poetic in that they communicate even before they are fully understood or analysed; indeed, they lift human communication to a new level. They are a proof if we need one that though we live in time, we are constantly being prompted to contemplate eternal realities. Hope is another of these words. It is an especially appropriate theme for Lent, when we recall the suffering and death of Jesus, spurred on by the sure hope of his resurrection. Born in us through

God's nearness, hope beckons us forward on the journey of faith.

To hope is to become aware of God's providence shaping our lives and guiding us through the ups and downs that are part and parcel of any life. In this book, I draw attention to the arts – music, painting, sculpture, poetry and story – as bridges of hope, and in the same light, I reflect on walking, on prayer and meditation, on love and laughter. Any or all of these bridges can, if we allow them, lead to hope. When fear threatens to drown our faith in God, during experiences when we are tempted to doubt God's love and care for us, the Holy Spirit renews in us the energy of hope, and makes us more alert to signs of hope that we can easily miss. Hope, a free gift of God, is a power for good, a blessing beyond price. It crystallizes our longings and brightens our lives. It reminds us that God is at the heart of our world, our universe, and that goodness is stronger than evil. You will find some of these thoughts and ideas in the chapters that follow.

'In difficult times,' wrote Blaise Pascal in his *Pensées*, 'carry something beautiful in your heart.' This Lent, with all that has been happening in our world, especially since 2020, when the coronavirus pandemic became a landmark in our lives, could that 'something beautiful' be hope? When a wave of hope rises in us, it gives us the courage to take new paths and tackle new tasks. Hope redresses the darkness that so often surrounds us, gently nudging us to seek and find God's presence even in unlikely situations, and opening our hearts and minds to the dream that lies at the heart of reality. Hope is a perceptible, effective sign of the presence of the Paraclete, the Comforter, who comes to help us in our weakness (Romans 8.26). It reminds us that at the heart of our failures and defeats, our disappointments and frustrations, God keeps us company.

Some people dread Lent, as I sometimes do myself, so, anticipating that it will be long and gloomy, should we just grit our teeth and look forward to Easter? But could there be an Easter without a Lent? Wildernesses, deserts, can be and often are considered negative environments, with their enforced austerity, and their lack of social amenities and normal human contact. Yet in the season of Lent, we respond to the Church's call to enter these places, to walk, with Jesus, the Way of the Cross. And at the end of those six weeks, nowhere is liturgical drama more haunting and eloquent than at the Easter Vigil, that Holy Night when our hopes are fulfilled, and we celebrate the indescribable mystery of the passing of Jesus from death to new life, marking the completion of the journey of the Christian community through the wilderness of Lent to the promised land of Easter.

Some years ago, in early January, during a cold spell in France, where I was living at the time, a weather bulletin on French television showed a line of eight or nine people mutely climbing a steep, icy mountain path — I think it was somewhere in the High Pyrenees. There was a sheer drop on one side and the viewer could see that the going was tough. Then the camera focused on a narrow side-track, and the leader smiled when he saw it. It led to an almost invisible aperture, like a portal, framed by bare, snow-laden branches of stunted trees on either side. The climbers passed through, and there below them was a steaming pool. They all ran towards it, removed their climbing boots, stripped off their outer clothing and entered the thermal waters with shouts of joy. I think the journalist said the surrounding temperature was -19 or -20 degrees Celsius ...

Remembering that scene, the arduous, silent journey and the ecstatic arrival, it seemed to me to be an image of Lent. For this liturgical season, moving towards its culmination, the celebration of Easter, encapsulates two symbols that are deeply rooted in the human imagination: wilderness and paradise. And hope – this was obvious in those climbers in the Pyrenees – is at the heart of the journey through the wilderness. Any wilderness, cold or hot, is filled with contradictions. At once frightening and fascinating, it offers the worst and the best of human experiences. It may be a place of sand and scorching sun, where there is sparse vegetation and little water, but it can also offer glimpses of unsuspected beauty. Or it may be a precipitous mountain, where 'winter and rough weather' render it all but inaccessible; and yet a seemingly barren, cold landscape can conceal surprising gifts, as was shown in that French television snippet. The journey is demanding, and with the travellers in danger of losing their way, wandering from the 'right' path can lead to a keen sense of abandonment, even to despair: will they ever reach their destination? Those who walk in this place of challenge may be faced not only with bewilderment, but also with hunger and thirst, with long, dark nights, with loneliness and silence. Is there light at the end of this tunnel? Are we really going to emerge into something better? Without hope, who could continue?

Waking up to a new day, as we get dressed and drink our first cup of tea or coffee, we usually find out what's going on by listening to the news. Some of it is good. Not too long ago, I read a newspaper article that gave statistics indicating that what the author called the 'giant evils' of poverty, hunger and disease were 'in headlong retreat' worldwide; it even cited Bill Gates as saying that poverty as we know it could be abolished in our lifetime. (Whether that journalist would say the same today, given the catastrophic effects of the coronavirus, is another matter.) We also know that there are many people from every nation under heaven who work unceasingly to build a more inclusive community in a more just and peaceful world, and they are doing so with even greater commitment in the aftermath of the pandemic. All this is good news indeed. There are many signs of hope, if we look at the world that is our home through God's eyes.

But it has to be said that it is bad news that often seems to predominate. We hear that ecological problems abound: in spite of recent efforts on the part of many individuals and countries, ice-caps are melting at an alarming rate, sea-levels are rising, glaciers receding. We listen uneasily to reports of wildfires and floods and droughts in different parts of the world; we hear that typhoons and earthquakes are expected to become increasingly frequent. We know that climate change is no longer a vague possibility; that not only human life on our planet but also animal and plant life is seriously endangered. The news drags on: epidemics, wars, towns and villages devastated, terrorist attacks, ethnic and religious clashes, people-trafficking, a thriving drugs trade, horrifying abuse of the young and the vulnerable, the spread of organized crime. Is this the kind of life we want to live? Is this the kind of world we want to pass on to our children: a threatened environment and deeply troubled human communities – a world where an existential anguish seems to float in the air we breathe?

On a personal level, too, many people complain that they are at the end of their tether; they feel empty and exhausted. I met someone recently who said she felt she was hanging on by the skin of her teeth; she just didn't know how she could go on. Her husband, almost blind and also hard of hearing, needed constant care. She herself was riddled with arthritis, and every movement was agonizing for her. I have known this woman – she is now in her mid-seventies – for many years, and I am keenly aware that in the last few months she has visibly lost much of her former vitality. That day, she seemed dispirited and downcast. Perhaps we think it's normal for middle-aged and elderly people to be like this, especially when they have to cope with severe physical or mental ailments in themselves or others, but medical journals report an enormous upsurge in depressive illnesses across the age groups, even among young children. Many people today seem to have lost the sense of the loving care of God for creation. They seem to be living without hope.

Where is God in all this turmoil and heartache? In pre-coronavirus days, when singing in church was a normal part of Sunday worship, I spent a weekend with some cousins in Milton Keynes and on the Sunday morning went to Mass with them in their parish church. It happened to be the feast of Christ the King, and as we took our places, someone was giving out printed hymn-sheets. When I saw the title of the entrance hymn, I was convulsed with the giggles and couldn't sing a note. It read: 'Our God resigns'! I looked round the congregation – the church was full – and saw that everyone was singing 'Our God reigns' with great enthusiasm, including my cousin

Mary and her family. I seemed to have been the only person who had noticed the theological error so boldly announced through that tiny typo!

It is true, of course, that today, even in matters of faith, we can often feel helpless and hopeless, so perhaps some people do indeed believe that our God has 'resigned', or, to use Nietzsche's words, that 'God is dead'. The Christian Churches are in disarray, and sometimes even strong believers hesitate to give much attention to what their leaders say. When they encourage us to seek ways of living together based on solidarity and respect for the whole of creation, we wonder how this could be accomplished, confronted as we are with unambiguous evidence of the sheer depth of our global problems, to say nothing of the dire effects of the pandemic, fake news and political shenanigans. What could we possibly do that would make a real difference to our damaged earth, the home we share with all created things? How could we put an end to warfare and pandemics? We do what we can to improve the lives of suffering and needy people, but there are so many we can never touch. We find ourselves questioning not only our Church but our faith in God, and it is clear that more and more young people simply dismiss the very idea of God.

Indeed, who knows what the future holds for people of faith in these times of doubt?

Against this background, an injection of hope is surely and sorely needed, and sometimes even to become aware of the need for hope, and to name it, is enough to nudge us into seeing and experiencing things more positively, more constructively. In an article published in the *Church Times* on 7 August 2020, in the week following the death of John Hume, the journalist Paul Vallely recalled interviewing Hume for *The Times* in the 1980s, at the height of the Troubles in Northern Ireland. He asked him why he repeatedly offered a more optimistic analysis of the situation in Ireland than events warranted. Hume replied: 'Always tell people that what you want to happen already *is* happening. Then you can be sure it *will* happen.' Vallely reflected that perhaps this wasn't optimism, but hope. It seems that if we long for change, we need to 'convey' the change, 'embody' it, in our words and actions.

In the Christian tradition, Lent is a time when we are invited to reflect more deeply on what is happening in our lives and, with God's help, to face the problems of life and resolve to do our bit in helping to build a better world. The aim of this book is to encourage us to do this in the context of hope, for hope brings transformation. Hope in this sense is not just wishful thinking, not just gritting our teeth and 'hoping for the best'. True hope is not a passive gift; we need to make appropriate efforts to obtain the things we hope for. Greta Thunberg could be a model for us here: some deep hope within her energizes her to imagine significant change in human behaviour regarding care of the earth, in spite of our unpromising record to date. I have heard that Greta does not publicly claim any religious faith or allegiance, and some people say she places her hope for environmental change in humanity rather than in God. Be that as it may, it is good to keep in mind that when we live in hope, we encounter the divine mystery. Through hope, which comes from God, we move from the reality of today to the dreams of tomorrow.

In Lent, as we reflect on these things, the Church invites us to anticipate the need for change in our lives, and if we are to change, we need to feel both the push of discomfort and the pull of hope. Hope challenges us not to miss God's wider vision for us and for our world. If our perspective is hopeful, we will begin to notice encouraging signs even in the midst of the confusion that often surrounds us, and we will not only notice but look out for signs of hope. Jonathan Sacks¹ says that hope is 'the best way, perhaps the only way, to retain our sense of the underlying goodness of the world and the miraculous gift of life itself'. Would it help if, during the weeks of Lent, we tried to keep our eyes and ears open so that we are more aware of the good people do? Would it help if we adverted to the fact that there are far more good Samaritans in this world than there are criminals and destroyers? And some of these people live in our own homes, our own streets, our own parish communities ...

In his letter to the Romans, St Paul beautifully expresses the reason for our hope:

Who will separate us from the love of Christ? Will hardship or distress, or persecution, or famine, or nakedness, or peril, or the sword? No ... For I am convinced that neither death, nor life, nor angels, nor rulers, nor things present, nor things to come, nor height, nor depth, nor anything else in all creation, will be able to separate us from the love of God in Christ Jesus our Lord. (Romans 8.35, 37-39)

Hope is a gift for life. It guides us not just through the weeks of Lent to the joy of Easter, but through other dreadful and dark situations, when we are not so sure of the outcome ...

PRAYER

O God,
during this time of Lent,
remind us of your nearness.
Teach us to discern signs of hope
in the reality of today.
Open our eyes
to see bridges of hope
leading to the dreams of tomorrow.
Open our ears
to hear the melody of hope
piping its constant song:
goodness is stronger than evil,
love is stronger than hate.
Open our hearts,
fill them with the energy of your Spirit,
that we may begin each day,
confident of your care

for us and for the whole of creation.
Lord, be with us,
in your love, be with us;
all our hope is in you.
Amen.

NOTE
At the end of each chapter, a few brief suggestions
will be offered, to aid personal reflection or group
discussion.

I

THE PROVIDENCE OF GOD

'Trust the past to God's mercy, the present to
God's love, and the future to God's providence.'

St Augustine

Divine providence is a biblical theme *par excellence*,
the entire drama of salvation being set against the
backcloth of the loving care of God for his Chosen
People. Belief in providence, however, was not
confined to the Hebrews or to the peoples of the
Middle East; it was widespread throughout the
ancient world, and is found in all races and nations,
and in all religions. In the West, many of the classical
Greek philosophers believed that 'God' (i.e. Zeus,
the supreme divinity of their pantheon), always
and everywhere present, watched over the world
and directed it according to his changeless decrees.
Later, Roman philosophers, such as Seneca, Marcus
Aurelius and Plotinus, inherited from the Greeks a

wealth of thinking on providence and regarded it as essential to any serious enquiry into the ultimate meaning of life. In the fourth century of our era, it was St Augustine of Hippo who brought divine providence into clear focus for Christianity. In doing so, he did not hesitate to modify what he had gleaned from the Greek and Roman thinkers. He taught that God, through his providence, shapes the course of history and leads the world towards the completion destined for it by the Creator. For him, providence represents God's presence in all of life, and it is rooted in the love God has for humanity and for the whole of creation.

The notion of providence communicates a caring presence, expressed through a compassionate 'humanness', which we interpret as God's loving engagement with our world. To be provident means to bless, to shelter, to give generously, to 'provide' (the root meaning of the word is to 'foresee') what is needed. Belief in providence, then, and the hope that flows from it, leads to a recognition that under God, often in spite of appearances to the contrary, there is a creative, saving purpose in everything that happens to us. This does not mean that providence is a facile, quick-fix remedy for every problem that confronts us. It is not simply glorified optimism or a vague feeling that everything will turn out all right in the end. In Christian terms, providence is linked with the virtue of hope: we place our trust in God, believing that he shapes and guides the advancement not only of humanity but of the whole cosmos. It means trusting that it is worthwhile to take the next steps on the untidy human journey because we can discern what St Augustine calls 'the footprints of God in creation'. In our time, living as we do amid global terrorism, pervasive conflict, pandemics and ecological degradation – and, for thousands of people in different parts of the world, crushing poverty and unjust structures – there could hardly be a more comforting message than encouragement to hope in the providence of God.

But, in practice, what does providence mean for us? How does God 'provide' for us? What is it that makes us hope for tangible marks of this providence – food when we're hungry, cures for our illnesses, care in our suffering, shelter when we're homeless, employment when we're jobless – especially when we know from experience that we're often going to be disappointed? How do we remain hopeful when this God we call provident seems deaf to our urgent pleas for demonstrable help? If love is at the heart of divine providence, which I believe it is, then perhaps the human evidence of that providence is our love for one another. In other words, it may be that God's way of providing for people in their need is to inspire us to be provident in our turn. Perhaps that is what we're all hoping for: that God's providence will be embodied in us. It could be said that here we have the essence of the spirit of the season of Lent: listening to God more attentively (prayer), choosing to do without some of our superfluities in order to seek a deeper understanding of our dependence upon God (fasting), and sharpening our practical concern for the poor and the weak (almsdeeds). When we do these things, we share God's provident desires by the way we care for one another while we wait in hope for the new life of Easter.

Yet it has to be said that there are times when we seem to inhabit a world in which the divine absence is often more obvious than the divine presence; times when many people, even believers, find it hard to accept the idea of a provident God. It is sometimes said that in today's world, God is missing, but not missed – and there is some truth in this. In this atmosphere, the gift of hope has an important role to play. Hope *does* miss God, seek God, long for God. Indeed, that is the very essence of hope: to feel the lack, the absence, the distance, and in spite of these things, to place our confidence in God. Psalm 116 puts it well: 'I trusted, even when I said, "I am greatly afflicted."' Hope offers a new vision, a new perspective on what is happening in the life of the world and in our own lives. It helps us to look beyond the immediate, to become more aware of what Milton called the 'goodness beyond thought' – which I think is his way of describing God's providence. Hope, which is an integral part of being human, trusts that all will be well, even in our present imperfection, and belief in providence is the fertile ground in which this virtue takes root. Faith in divine providence gives birth in us to what John Clare in one of his poems calls the *instinct* of hope, by which we truly trust in God even in the face of doubts and reservations and temptations to despair. Hope, with faith as its starting point and love as its guiding light, leads us, once we have done our best to bring about change where change is needed, to be at peace with what happens to us, believing that all of life, past, present and future, is held in God's loving hands.

'Learn from yesterday, live for today, hope for tomorrow,' said Einstein. Faith is silently sustaining; it draws attention to the way things have been. Love is active; it highlights the way things are, knows that the power of God is already effective in our lives. Hope is alert, open to surprises, and ready to step into the unknown; it points to the way things will be. Hope in providence means trusting that the destructive forces within us and in our world can never break the bond that connects us with the everlasting love of God. This does not mean forcing ourselves to hope against hope in every situation, because, as we know only too well, there are situations in which there is no hope. Paul Tillich, a Lutheran theologian who wrote extensively on Christian hope, gives a few examples of such apparently hope-less situations: 'when death rains from heaven as it does now, when cruelty wields power over nations and individuals as it does now, when hunger and persecution drive millions from place to place as they do now, when prisons and slums all over the world distort the humanity of souls and bodies as they do now'.[1] But, he adds, even in times like these, *especially* in times like these, hope in providence confirms in us what we know in our hearts: that nothing can separate us from the love of

God, and that ultimately all things will work together for good.

Trust in God's providence is beautifully expressed in the words of Jesus: 'Are not two sparrows sold for a penny? Yet not one of them will fall to the ground apart from your Father' (Matthew 10.29). Dietrich Bonhoeffer (a contemporary of Tillich and also a Lutheran theologian) makes an interesting comment on this verse: 'not everything that happens to us is the will of God, yet in the last resort nothing happens without his will, i.e., through every event, however untoward, there is always a way through to God'.[2] Condemned because of his open opposition to Nazism, Bonhoeffer was writing these words from prison, unsure of the fate that awaited him. Yet he clearly believed that from any evil we may experience, God can and does draw good, even if, humanly speaking, the situation seems desperate and irremediable. Through hope, we cherish an inner conviction that God, in his providence, writes straight on crooked lines. Providence is God's faithful love watching over all that happens to us and to our world.

Sometimes a gruelling, painful or frustrating experience can be 'redeemed' by writing about it, talking about it, singing about it. Some of the songs of the slaves in seventeenth- and eighteenth-century America illustrate in a deeply touching way that belief in God's providence was, for those suffering people, the only way they could endure the affliction that was their lot. They found comfort in pondering the brutal death of Jesus on the cross, and in doing so, they glimpsed hope and resurrection amid the horror of his suffering and of their own. I am reminded of one of those songs, whose words, minimal though they are, seem to express both trust in God's providence and hope of resurrection:

> Nobody knows the trouble I've seen
> Nobody knows but Jesus
> Nobody knows the trouble I've seen
> Glory, halleluiah!

In those terrible years, slavery was not confined to America. It is true that huge numbers of black people in America, shamefully referred to and treated as 'slaves', spent their lives in appalling situations, picking cotton. But in eighteenth-century England, where this cotton was processed in the first industrialized textile factories, working conditions were also grim in the extreme. The cotton mills – William Blake called them 'these dark satanic mills' – may have provided much-needed employment, but sadly the thousands of men, women and children who worked in them, twelve hours a day, six days a week, were little more than 'slaves' in their turn.

Dating from a slightly later period, another song, 'Land of Heart's Desire', also sprang from a background of unrelenting manual labour, poverty and injustice, if not outright slavery, this time in the Hebrides, during the Highland Clearances. This song (translated from the Gaelic by Marjory Kennedy-Fraser), with its beautiful title and melody, is an ecstatic hymn giving expression to the Hebridean hope of heaven. It is a song that illustrates the truth of the perceptive words of H. A. Williams: 'Lent is but Easter in disguise'. No doubt, similar songs are being composed and sung and hummed today by victims of modern slavery and by others who suffer at the hands of thugs, abusers and people-traffickers, or as a result of wars, pandemics, natural disasters or climate change in our time. Their belief in the immensity of God's providence can lead them to wait on God and to hope for new life, for resurrection, in the midst of their suffering. For them, hope is an indispensable companion on the journey of life.

If we see God's providence as the backdrop of our lives, it is amazing how we can find small scraps of hope even in times of desperation and fear, seeds of wisdom even in unwanted experiences and unwelcome happenings. Does hope also mean believing in small, modest, 'everyday' miracles? Some would say it does. The twentieth-century German theologian, Karl Rahner, SJ, had a deeply contemplative approach to the mystery of God as revealed in our ordinary human experiences. Once, when he was asked whether he believed in miracles, he replied that he didn't *believe* in them, he *counted on* them to get through each day. Having a keen sense of divine providence in his life, he saw the finger of God in the apparently chance events, good and bad, that come to us all. To him, these everyday experiences were 'miracles' because they spoke to him of God's guiding presence in life. It was not that he believed God deliberately made such things happen – nature, luck, human freedom, human sinfulness, coincidence could have caused them – but for him they were more than simply a conspiracy of accidents; they were a source of hope, of confidence in God's presence in his life. And hope is always miraculous ...

Miracles, small and great, can put us in touch with aspects of life that we often miss or overlook. They startle us into a clearer consciousness of God's presence, and they keep alive in us the amazement that is vital in our relationship with God. God's goodness is beyond our understanding, and we can be blind to the wonders that surround us; and then, out of the blue, something happens that sharpens our vision. Many years ago, in a book by Ronald Rolheiser, OMI,[3] I read an account of a true experience that clearly illustrates how an apparent conspiracy of accidents can be seen, and in this case was seen, as an intervention of God in a person's life, in other words, a 'miracle'. I have never forgotten that story, and I quote it here with the author's permission. During my long years of teaching, I told and retold it in countless RE classes, and I always found that the students, all of them, responded positively to the story – they could readily appreciate its meaning. The woman concerned had been brought up in a religious home and had been a regular churchgoer, but admitted that during her student years her faith had lapsed, adding that for several years after graduation she no longer attended church or prayed at all. But then, something happened that changed things for her:

One day, four years after having given up all practice of prayer and church, she flew to Colorado to spend some time with a married sister and to do some skiing. She arrived on a Saturday evening and the next morning, Sunday, her sister invited her to go to Mass with her. She politely refused and went skiing instead. On her first run down the ski-slope she hit a tree and broke her leg. Sporting a huge cast, she was released from hospital the following Saturday. The next morning, her sister again invited her to come to Mass with her. This time ('there wasn't anything else to do') she accepted the invitation. As luck would have it, it was Good Shepherd Sunday. As chance would have it, there happened to be a priest visiting from Israel. He could not see her, complete with cast, sitting in the pews and yet he began his sermon this way: 'There is a custom among shepherds in Israel that existed at the time of Jesus and is still practised today that needs to be understood in order to appreciate this text. Sometimes very early on in the life of a lamb, a shepherd senses that it is going to be a congenital stray, one forever drifting away from the herd. What that shepherd does then is to take the lamb and deliberately break its leg so that he has to carry it until its leg is healed. By that time, the lamb has become so attached to the shepherd that it never strays again!' 'I may be dense,' said this woman, 'but, given my broken leg and all this chance coincidence, hearing this woke something up inside me. Fifteen years have passed since then, and I have prayed and gone to church regularly ever since.'

Rolheiser concludes: 'What this woman experienced that Sunday was precisely the language of God, divine providence, God's finger in her life, through a conspiracy of accidents.' I have to say that although the details of this story are far, very far, from my personal experience (I have never been to the United States, let alone to Colorado, have never been skiing, and, so far, have never broken my leg!), I was struck by the woman's readiness to allow herself to be touched by what she heard. I found it a hopeful story, and for me, as for her, its meaning is crystal clear: we can encounter the mystery of God's providence in the concrete happenings of our everyday lives.

Because many people respond more fully to the idea of the providence of God when it comes to us through the hands of a mother, one of the popular depictions of Mary in Christian art is as the tender, compassionate Mother of Mercy, sheltering people under her outspread cloak. Gerard Manley Hopkins, in his poem 'The Blessed Virgin compared to the Air we Breathe', sees her in this guise:

> She, wild web, wondrous robe,
> Mantles the guilty globe.

She is the one who surrounds us all with the 'air' of mercy:

> ... we are wound
> With mercy round and round
> As if with air.

He goes on to say that Mary is the one whom God 'has let dispense ... his providence', and she does this through her prayers of loving concern for the whole of creation. Mary brings God into our orbit; she is the 'world-mothering air' that surrounds us. The opening verses of the letter to the Hebrews speak of Christ as 'the radiant light of God's glory ... sustaining the universe by his powerful command'. But for Mary, that 'glory bare' would blind us, so her hand providently 'sifts' the radiant light 'to suit our sight'; and she does this because of her motherly sensitivity to our needs.

Faith in divine providence, like other aspects of faith in God, is expressed in a variety of ways, symbolically and verbally, in different parts of the world. I recently spent three years in Paris, and I was fascinated to discover pictures of the Eye of God, representing providence, in a number of churches. Interestingly, one such picture can be seen in St Aloysius Roman Catholic Church in Somers Town, London, a stone's throw from Euston Station. The earliest church on that site was built for French émigrés who came to London in the aftermath of the 1789 Revolution, and these people must have been reassured to see a familiar representation of divine providence in the church where they worshipped during their years of exile. In the history corner at the back of the present church, that same picture of the Eye of God is given pride of place: a large, unblinking blue eye, vividly portrayed with stylized eyelid and eyelashes and framed in a triangle representing the Trinity, continues to look down upon all those who enter that part of the church. Did this picture have a biblical origin? Many of the Psalms seem to indicate that it probably did, but here a single verse from Psalm 11 will suffice to illustrate the importance of this image of a provident God who cares for his creation: 'God's eyes behold the world; his gaze probes the children of men' (v. 4).

The Hand of God is another favoured symbol of providence in many cultures, and it, too, is beautifully articulated in the Psalms. Psalm 139 is a good example: 'If I take the wings of the dawn, or dwell at the seas furthest end, even there your hand would lead me, your right hand would hold me fast' (vv. 9-10). The seventeenth-century French preacher Bossuet, who devoted several of his sermons to divine providence, expressed it like this: 'The hand of God is too clearly manifested in our lives for us not to recognise it.' The Eye of God and the Hand of God, these two classic symbols of the providence of God, both became more meaningful for me during that immersion into French culture. Through them, I came to see more clearly that belief in providence is the source of our hope.

While in France, I also developed a fondness for the phrase *le bon Dieu*, which seems to encapsulate a spirituality that has its source in a deep awareness of divine providence, and this, for many people, even today, is at the heart of their journey of faith. It is often said that the number of committed Christians in France, as elsewhere in Europe and in other parts of the world, is, in our times, diminishing year on year. No doubt this is true, but during those years in Paris, I noticed that many French people, even in ordinary conversation, still seem to refer to God quite naturally as *le bon Dieu* – indeed, it seems to be an everyday term. For me, this impression was confirmed one day in a local supermarket when I heard an exchange between an elderly customer and a young cashier. Apparently, the man had mislaid his credit card and was finding it very inconvenient to be obliged to use his wife's. Insisting that he had not really *lost* the card, he was complaining that he just did not know where he had put it. 'Why don't you ask *le bon Dieu* to help you?' said the cashier, quietly joining her hands and bowing her head. I don't know if this was a typical French response, but I relished it.

From the way the phrase is used in French, *le bon Dieu* seems to denote the first person of the Trinity, the Father, often seen as the omnipotent Creator God. But the 'face' of this person is not grandly remote, commanding and punitive; it is, above all, good and kind. I am reminded of Bernadette Farrell's song, 'Everyday God', where there is a similar blending of transcendence and immanence. In that song, which is a kind of litany, at the start of each verse, the first person of the Trinity is variously addressed as 'Earth's creator', as 'Life of all lives', as 'Our beginning'; but the refrain is always the same: 'Everyday God'. That everyday God is present in the joys and sorrows of life and living; the God who is beyond us is also among us as a friend, a companion. I have a sense that it is in the context of a trustful, affectionate relationship with God that the expression *le bon Dieu* is used in French, and that belief in divine providence is the foundation of this relationship.

It is true that *le bon Dieu* does not translate easily into English. Literally, of course, we could say the words mean 'the good God', but that would be to pass over the spirit behind the words, and 'spirit' is notoriously untranslatable. Spirit can be sensed, felt, but not adequately expressed in words – although it must be said that in poetry as in prayer, words can be spirit-filled. As I write that, I find myself wondering if perhaps the tiny phrase, *le bon Dieu*, is in truth a poetic expression that carries us into the heart of God's *tendresse*, into the realm of divine goodness and truth and beauty … Is that the reason for its perennial allure? When we turn to *le bon Dieu*, when we entrust our lives to God's providence, do we touch the hand of the eternal? As St Paul said to the Council of the Areopagus, 'God is not far from each of us, for in him we live and move and have our being' (Acts 17.27-28). *Le bon Dieu* is indeed closer to us than the ground we stand on, and if we take time to listen, God's voice, God's music, the melody of hope, filters through the noise of our lives, bringing love and promise.

In the prayer we call 'The Lord's Prayer', Jesus seems to be drawing our attention to the providence of God, and he expresses this through the notion of the fatherhood of God. Jesus was very fond of the word *Father* – it is by far his most frequent term for God. He was Jewish, and *Father* is one of the words the Jews have always used to speak of God or to address God, and often Christians like to do the same. Is 'Father' a good image, a meaningful metaphor for God? It is of course only one of our many ways of referring to God, and sadly not everyone can relate to it positively because they have not experienced the kind of fatherhood Jesus seems to take for granted. However, when we *do* use this word to speak of God or to God, are we implying that human parents, at their best, are a bit like God? Are we saying that we can speak to God as freely as we would speak to a loving father or mother? In our hearts, we know that God is not just a celestial cleaner-up of messes and sorter-out of problems, but when we see him as father or mother, we can sometimes find within ourselves the resources to cope and to hope. Because we know we can count on God's providential care, we are better able to put things into perspective and move forward in spite of the confusion that often surrounds us. We sense that God is with us in our difficulties, giving us an inner peace and a hope that enables us to live with or handle those difficulties, and even to surmount them.

Jesus seems to be saying in effect that we can turn to God as easily as we turn to a good father or mother. When he taught his disciples this prayer – and it is significant that the first word is *OUR* – he was recognizing all people as his brothers and sisters under God. In the same way, we ourselves, using Jesus' words, unite ourselves with all people, believers or unbelievers, who are part of God's family – perhaps that is why many people extend their hands in a gesture of inclusion when they say the 'Our Father'. I once met a missionary priest who had spent many years in the Solomon Islands in Oceania, and he told

me that in the pidgin English version of the Lord's
Prayer used by the people there, the first words are,
'*Papa bilong youmifella*' (if you read those three words
aloud, you cannot fail to understand them!). What a
wonderful way to begin the prayer that Jesus taught
us: Papa (Jesus would have said 'Abba', an affectionate
diminutive of 'father') belongs to you and to me.
The implication is that when we say 'Our Father', we
leave individualism behind. We pray with and for one
another, for the community, for everyone, not just for
ourselves, praising God and asking him to attend to
not only our needs but the needs of everyone else too.
God's loving providence knows no bounds, and by
addressing God as *Our* Father, Jesus is teaching us that
nobody can approach God as if he or she is an only
child. We are brothers and sisters in God's family; we
belong to God and to one another.

Our God is not a mighty creator who made the
world and then (like some of the gods of the ancient
Greeks and the Romans) takes little further interest in
it. God is like good human parents, who love and care
for their children, and he wants a relationship with
them, for they are the work of his hands. We feel safe
with a good father and mother; they brought us into
the world, and they cared for us day after day. They

fed us and taught us and protected us; they helped us grow to adulthood. Yet although we call on God as we call on a parent, father or mother, we know that these words do not describe God fully. Indeed, God is profoundly different from all the parents we know. He is a Father 'in heaven', hidden from our natural perception, and 'heaven' is a word we use to speak of something completely above us, something beyond our grasp. As Jesuit David Toolan says:

> for the most part it is only when purpose or providence or love is embodied, when it takes on a face or name – and speaks our name – that we can trust it. For Christians, Jesus Christ is that embodiment, God's eternal Word – in the flesh – telling us that 'God loved the world so much that he gave his only Son, so that everyone who believes in him may not be lost but may have eternal life.'[4]

Jesus, as I knew from my earliest childhood, had called himself 'the Good Shepherd' (there was a picture of him in my primary school assembly hall), but I have to confess that, until I saw Elisabeth Frink's bronze sculpture, *Pater Noster*, I had never really thought of God the Father as a shepherd. Yet that is what the sculptor seems to suggest by giving her piece that title. She was responding, I imagine, to the setting for which the piece was commissioned in 1975, Paternoster Square, beside St Paul's Cathedral in the City of London. In doing so, she was no doubt inspired by biblical imagery, which represents God as the Shepherd of Israel, but she may also have been keeping in mind the original, very mundane purpose of this Square, which in Victorian times was the site of the Newgate meat market. According to her obituary in *The Times*, Frink concentrated on three essential themes in her work: the human form, the 'horseness' of horses, and touches of the divine in human life and living. It seems to me it could be said that all three themes appear in this group. The figure of the shepherd depicts humanity at its noblest: the shepherd is plainly strong, upstanding and caring. There are no horses here, but the five sheep are unmistakably sheep – there is something about that little flock that, to me at least, epitomizes the 'sheepness' of sheep: their trust in the shepherd, their docility, their contentment in ambling along together. As for the third theme, touches of the divine in human life and living, this is summed up for me in a verse from the prophet Micah

(5.4): 'He shall stand and feed his flock in the strength of the Lord, in the majesty of the name of the Lord his God. And they shall live secure ...' Perhaps this was Elisabeth's main inspiration? It is in Pater Noster, in God's providential care for us and for our world, that we place our hope.

Hope embraces the whole of reality, and reality includes the true and the good, the faltering and the imperfect. When we do not know what we should hope for, the Spirit comes to help us in our weakness. When the future is uncertain or unpredictable, we call on God, as we would call on a loving father or mother, to provide for us, and we hope for a favourable response. We hope for a better world, trusting in the faithfulness and loving kindness of God, and at the same time trying, for our part, to make this better, fairer world become a reality. We take refuge in God, we place our enduring hope in God's promises, but when to our disappointment things do not turn out as we desire and expect, we have to acknowledge that God's ways are not our ways. It is then that we have to learn to say, trusting in God's providence, 'Your will, not mine, not ours, be done.' And as we wait in hope for God's reign to come 'on earth as it is in heaven', we continue to pray for justice, for peace, for healing, for courage.

The human person is indestructible, and even death does not put an end to God's provident care for each one of us. A few years ago, I heard a story about a seven-year-old Scottish boy who wrote a letter to his dead father and confidently posted it. On the envelope he had written: 'Mister Postman, please can you take this to paradise for my daddy's birthday? Thank you.' In the sorting office, one of the postal workers, on reading this message, was deeply touched. He waited a few days, then he sent a reply to the little boy: 'We have managed to deliver your letter to your daddy in heaven. As you can imagine, it was quite a challenge for us to dodge the stars and other galactic objects on the journey to paradise, but we made it, and it's now in his hands.' The child had no doubts: his father would read that birthday letter. He believed in the providence of God, and, by the instinct of hope, knew intuitively that death does not signal the end of human existence, that love never comes to an end. The postal worker sounds as if he was prepared to believe it too. Gabriel Marcel said it well: 'To love someone is to say to him or to her: you will not die.'[5]

FOR PERSONAL REFLECTION OR GROUP DISCUSSION

1 Do you believe in everyday miracles?
2 How do you respond to the deep faith in the providence of God as expressed in the 'spirituals' of the African slaves of seventeenth- and eighteenth-century America?
3 Would you use an image like the 'Hand of God' to refer to certain experiences in your own life?

FURTHER SUGGESTIONS

1 Read and ponder 'The Instinct of Hope' by John Clare.
2 Invite a deaf friend to teach you how to 'sign' the Lord's Prayer. Notice how using hand movements can help you to enter more deeply into the prayer that Jesus taught us.
3 Hum, sing or play a recording of one of the 'spirituals' of the African American slaves.

2

GOODNESS IS STRONGER
THAN EVIL

'It is a characteristic of God to overcome evil
with good.'

Julian of Norwich

Reading the newspapers, checking the news headlines
on our phones and PCs, listening to news programmes
on the radio or watching them on television, we may
feel that things are going badly wrong in human
life and living. Indeed, we could sometimes get the
impression that most people in this world of ours
are violent thugs, drug pushers, abusers, terrorists
or thieves. But from our own experience, we know
this is not true. So, against the background of all that
is going on in our world, perhaps the weeks of Lent
will be more hopeful if we keep Julian's words (see
above) to the forefront of our minds, believing, as
she did, that God is with us on the journey of life.

Many people (probably, if the truth were known, most people) sincerely try to lead a good life, and usually they do this without drawing undue attention to themselves. They are kind, compassionate and ready to help others, especially those in distress or any kind of need. This has been confirmed many times in the past months, ever since the coronavirus first began to infect our world. These good people respect the rights of others, they are always ready to give a helping hand, and insofar as they can (prodded, perhaps, by David Attenborough's documentaries or Prince William's Earthshot project), they try to make care of the planet one of their priorities. Of course, they sometimes fail, as we all do, but in general their lives show that their hearts are in the right place: they treat other people with courtesy, try to avoid doing harm to anyone or anything, and are often incredibly generous and kind. It really is true: goodness is stronger than evil.

God alone can hold together the mysteries of life, the seeming contradictions that we all experience, the perplexing juxtaposition of goodness and wickedness that we see around us. Why should evil be part of our lives, troubling us, threatening us, harming us? There is no easy answer to this question, for evil is a mystery.

Evil, wickedness, whether we witness it or suffer from it personally, whether we hear about it or read about it, can cause surprise and shock, fear, revulsion or anger. But isn't it true that, at the end of the day, evil and evil people have no lasting attraction? They leave us cold and desolate. But goodness, the sheer giftedness of life, is a mystery too. Why should people be good, especially when, personally, they seem to gain little or nothing by their good actions? However, unlike evil, goodness draws us like a magnet. When Wordsworth speaks of the 'little, nameless, unremembered acts of kindness and of love' that represent the best part of anyone's life, he seems to imply that good people do their good deeds instinctively, spontaneously, and don't even remember doing them. Yet a truly good person is never forgotten. Rabbi Jonathan Sacks, having officiated at countless funeral services, was keenly aware of this. 'The people who were the most mourned,' he noticed,

were not the richest, or the most famous, or the most successful. They were people who enhanced the lives of others. They were kind. They were loving. They had a sense of their responsibilities. When they could, they gave to charitable causes.

If they could not give money, they gave time. They were loyal members of communities. They were people you could count on. [1]

Genuine goodness touches something deep inside us and, when we meet it, it fills us with hope. It warms us, inspires us, moves us to respond to life in a positive way. Good people, without any apparent effort, leave a trail of light behind them. In that light we see the way we ought to go, the way we want to go, and we feel a strong pull in that direction. Such people encourage us to choose the good, to walk with them along the 'right' path, the path of faith and hope and love. This does not mean of course that good people have no problems, that they are protected from the suffering or anxiety that is part of our common human inheritance. It would be a false picture to see them as always completely secure in their faith, full of undying hope, showing their love for everyone they meet by their kind actions, and cheerfully striding through life with a clear sense that God is always at their side. They too have their moments, long moments perhaps, of desolation; they too have to face serious setbacks and personal anguish. But when, in desperation, they reach the end of their tether, they turn to God in prayer, longing for God's nearness, longing for a glimmer of light in the darkness that surrounds them.

Hope, trust in God, enables us to bear inevitable pain and suffering with patience, even when it is unjustly inflicted, and to come through it without losing heart. When Martin Luther King Jr experienced a deep sense of doubt and darkness in his life, he said that the only thing that upheld him was prayer. It seems that one night, at the height of his struggle for civil rights for black people in America, he felt completely overwhelmed. He and his family had received so many insults and threats of serious injury that he felt he could not go on; he had reached rock bottom. In a state of physical and mental exhaustion, he threw himself on his knees and prayed: 'Lord, I have taken a stand for what I believe is right. But now I am afraid. The people are looking to me for leadership. If I stand before them without strength or courage, they too will falter. But I am at the end of my powers. I have nothing left. I've come to the point where I can't face it alone.' It was at that moment of near-despair that a spark of hope was kindled in him, and because of that spark he found the inner strength to continue the struggle. 'Darkness,' he said, 'cannot drive out darkness: only light can do that. Hate cannot drive out hate: only love can do that.' Sustained by prayer, he was able to hope that, ultimately, goodness and love would triumph over evil and hate. Archbishop Desmond Tutu's little prayer echoes King's words:

> Goodness is stronger than evil;
> Love is stronger than hate;
> Light is stronger than darkness;
> Life is stronger than death;
> Victory is ours through Him who loves us.

Like Martin Luther King Jr and Desmond Tutu, many people of faith learn, with God's help, to keep hold of hope, to hang on to it, sometimes by the skin of their teeth, trusting that the darkness around them, thick though it may be, will never totally crush their spirit. These incorrigible hopers, like Elijah in his cave, learn to listen, as Jim Cotter says in his *Prayer at Night*, 'to the fragile feelings, not to the clashing fury, to the quiet sounds, not to the loud clamour, to the steady heartbeat, not to the noisy confusion, to the hidden voices, not to the obvious chatter, to the deep harmonies, not to the surface discord'. They believe that God is with them even when he seems distant. Hope makes them attentive to the signs of God's presence, and they find themselves able to discern sparkles of light in the shadows of night. It is this desire and readiness to recognize God's presence, even in unpromising circumstances, that makes a good life, a truly 'virtuous' life. The virtuous are dedicated to what St Ignatius of Loyola, in a well-known phrase, calls *finding God in all things*. They are tuned in to the nearness of God, and so the direction and rhythm of their lives is transformed by the energy of the Spirit. As we know only too well, life is not always affirming and joyful, and indeed sorrow and joy are not too distant from each other, but the Spirit brings hope, a sense of being held by God at the deepest centre of our being. Even when everything in our lives seems to be falling apart, hope holds out the promise of redemption.

Leading a good life and living in hope is not a purely theoretical matter; we can see it embodied in actual people in their efforts to 'act justly, love tenderly and walk humbly with God' (Micah 6.8). This was movingly illustrated during some of the hearings of the Truth and Reconciliation Commission that took place in South Africa after the national policy of apartheid had come to an end in 1990. The Anglican priest and author, Chris Chivers, who had been present at one such hearing, recounts the following true story:

I am sitting in the civic hall in Guguletu, a Cape Town township community, in November 1996. A 70-year-old woman has been called to testify before South Africa's Truth and Reconciliation Commission concerning the activities of a policeman in her township. It transpires that he had come one night with some others and in front of the woman had shot her son at point-blank range. Two years later the same officer had returned to arrest her husband, whom she supposed subsequently to have been executed. Some time later, the policeman came yet again. This time he took her to a place where he showed her her husband, still alive. But as her spirits lifted, the policeman doused the husband with gasoline, set him on fire and killed him. As the woman concludes her testimony, the presiding officer addresses her: 'What would you like the outcome to be of this hearing?' After a long pause, the woman answers, 'I would like three things. First, I want to be taken to the place where my husband was burned, so I can gather up the dust and give his remains a decent burial. Second, my son and my husband were my only family. Therefore, I want this police officer to become my son, to come twice a month to my home and spend a day with me so I can pour out on him whatever love I still have remaining inside me. Finally, I want this officer to know that I offer him forgiveness because Jesus Christ died to forgive me. Please would someone lead me across the hall so that I can embrace him and let him know that he is truly forgiven.'[2]

In the midst of the intense suffering and injustice she had faced all her life, this woman was sustained by her love for Jesus, and because of that, she was able to meet devastating hatred with overwhelming love. Perhaps she knew instinctively that when an injury is done to us, we never recover until we learn to forgive. And perhaps she discovered, like C. S. Lewis, that 'God whispers to us in our pleasures, but shouts in our pain.' Jesus' example led her to forgive the man who had brutally taken from her the two persons who were most dear to her in all the world. She was under no illusions: her husband and son, her only child, would never return to her, yet her trust in God's providence remained unbroken and absolute.

She hungered and thirsted for what is right, and she was satisfied, knowing that nothing and no one could ever separate her from the love of God. In a spirit of hope, she awaited the coming of God's kingdom, the new world of justice and truth and peace, and she was ready to play her part in building this kingdom by uniting her pain with the sufferings of Jesus, and by forgiving her enemies as he had forgiven his.

Lent, and especially Holy Week, when we recall the suffering and death of Jesus, offers us a powerful reminder that suffering cannot be side-stepped. Yet this does not mean there is no way through it: healing comes from entering into the pain and waiting on God. Opening up in hope to the experience of helplessness leads to the discovery that God will find us, meet us, in our sorrow and distress. 'I pray that the God of our Lord Jesus Christ, the Father of glory, may give you a spirit of wisdom and revelation as you come to know him, so that, with the eyes of your heart enlightened, you may know what is the hope to which he has called you' (Ephesians 1.17, 18). The Guguletu hearing, as reported by Chris Chivers, places centre stage a frail elderly woman whose inward eyes were illumined by hope. Hope gave her the strength to endure unspeakably tragic, deeply damaging experiences without losing heart, even to the point of being determined, against all the odds, to seek reconciliation with the person who had wronged her. Her example shows that when hope glows at the centre of our lives, warmth and respect unfold in us, hatred and violence recede. Goodness is stronger than evil ...

The cross is where believers find a God who is vulnerable. Jesus, the Son of God, submitted to crucifixion, a death usually reserved for slaves and rebels, and his life on earth ended in disgrace and apparent failure. The devotion of the Stations of the Cross is a prayerful, contemplative way of engaging with the suffering and death of Jesus. It is a practice inspired by the hope of life after death, a hope that is gloriously fulfilled in the resurrection of Jesus. In the early years of Christianity, and for many centuries afterwards, pilgrims, often at great cost to themselves and their families, would travel long distances and encounter many dangers in order to get to Jerusalem. Here their aim was to walk in the footsteps of Jesus as he carried his cross on his last journey. When, in medieval times, wars or plagues prevented Christians from travelling to the Holy Land, the 14 Stations of the Cross, based on scripture and pious tradition, offered people the possibility of undertaking a mini-pilgrimage to Calvary. Gradually, from about the fifteenth century, pictures or sculptures representing the traditional 'stations' (stopping places) of Jesus on his last journey began to be put up in many churches and, later, out of doors. As time went on, a Lenten ritual developed: the priest, accompanied by acolytes and moving from station to station, would read an appropriate meditation on each incident. There would be time for silent reflection, the singing of a refrain – usually some lines from the *Stabat Mater* – and the 'pilgrims' would join in prayers and responses.

The desire to contemplate the sufferings of Jesus is at the heart of this devotion: 'All you who pass this way, look and see: is there any sorrow like the sorrow that afflicts me?' (Lamentations 1.12). The spiritual writer, John O'Donoghue, was of the opinion that the contemplative mind, through what he calls 'the gaze of tenderness', courageously endeavours to turn the bleakness of death into a welcoming gentleness. In this way, the shadow of death becomes shot through with a beautiful light, like a bright star shining in a clear, dark sky. 'When the heart finds its contemplative radiance,' he wrote, 'the darkness of death shall have no dominion.' Psalm 84 has the same message: those who live in

God's house, sustained by God's presence in their lives, are just as likely as anyone else to experience suffering and pain, but 'as they go through the bitter valley, they make it a place of springs; they walk with ever-growing strength' (vv. 6-7). That 'ever-growing strength' is the energy of hope; hope that beyond the agony and shame of the cross, beyond the horror of the brutality of the death of Jesus, there is new life. Our horizons, limited by death, are not God's horizons. After death there is the promise of eternal life.

If this is true, and I believe it is, it is not surprising to find that Julian of Norwich, like other contemplative souls, sees no need to be afraid of death. For her, death and life are one in God; goodness is stronger than evil, love is stronger than death, light is stronger than darkness. She herself fearlessly encountered the abyss, and returned with images of hope and love and healing. She discovered that a blessing rests on those whose lives are full of pain and sorrow, and believed that, if they face into their suffering in God's presence, they will be comforted. Through her contemplation of the Passion of Jesus, Julian came to the realization that God does not abandon us in the anguish and cruelty that we ourselves inflict, endure or see others endure. Her trust never wavered: God's love is always there, with us and for us, in and through it all. Hope pours light into the darkness of suffering, for it reaches out to God and discovers that God lightens the load by sharing it with us.

Julian lived in a tumultuous age: the Hundred Years' War was still going on, and fourteenth-century Europe was experiencing enormous political unrest and social upheaval. The Church too was in disarray, and was deeply involved in power struggles and warfare. At home in England, death was known personally to the population at large not only through the loss of thousands during the long years of the war, but also through the bubonic plague, the so-called Black Death, which swept through Norwich three times during Julian's lifetime. Few if any families would have been unaffected and all would have known great sadness and hardship through the deaths of relatives, friends and neighbours. Julian does not speak of the plague directly (nor of any other social or political events) but her book shows a deep sensitivity to suffering and dying, not least in her persistent questioning of why suffering should be permitted at all in a universe loved by God.

When Julian was 30 years old (she engagingly tells us her exact age, thirty and a half!), she became seriously ill. She was believed to be on the verge of death when, one day, quite suddenly, all the pain left her and she had a series of mystical visions – she called them 'showings' – which had as their central focus the Passion of Jesus. These visions gave Julian a deep awareness of what she calls 'the homely love of her courteous Lord', a love that gave her much joy, inner peace, hope and courage. She tells us in her book that the visions followed the visit of a priest, who brought her a crucifix. This he set before her, saying: 'I have brought the image of your Saviour; look at it and take comfort from it.' She admits that it was hard for her to look steadfastly at the cross: 'At this time I wanted to look away from the cross, but I did not dare, for I knew well that whilst I contemplated the cross, I was secure and safe.' It was a transformative experience for her, and she spent the rest of her life pondering the visions and writing about them in her book, *Showing of Love*. It is in that book that she articulates her theology of hope, beautifully summarized in Jesus' words to her: 'I may make all things well, I can make all things well and I will make all things well, and I shall make all things well, and you shall see yourself that all manner of thing shall be well' (Chapter 31).

Suffering is a universal human experience, and no one can escape it. It is a problem that Julian faces head on, and her hope-filled insights on this mystery have an amazingly contemporary ring. Her words are an encouragement to us not to be afraid to confront the evil and suffering in our world and in our own hearts, but to allow God to lead us heavenward through it. For her, these are truths more real, more authentic, than any passing emotions or feelings we may have. She tells us that God's love is present as much in hurt and suffering as it is in joy and gladness. When our whole world breaks up around us, when we experience loneliness and depression, when physical or mental pain take hold of us, she says that it is good to remember that God is with us in it all. Then we can pray with the Psalmist, as Julian did: 'Why are you cast down, my soul; why groan within me? Hope in God; I will praise him still, my Saviour and my God' (Psalm 42.5, 11).

It is heartening to listen to Julian, who in her visions has been to heaven, and has come back filled with the wisdom of God. She teaches us to be receptive, and for her, receptivity means creatively waiting on God. There is empowerment in the waiting: it means living in hope, the hope of future glory. Without meaning, suffering can destroy us, but if we find a meaning in it, it can transform us. Julian was shown that love was the meaning:

> I desired oftentimes to know what was our Lord's meaning [in times of sorrow and darkness]. And fifteen years after and more I was answered in ghostly understanding, saying thus, 'Would you know your Lord's meaning in this thing? Know it well, love was his meaning. Who showed it to you? Love. What did he show you? Love. Why did he show it to you? For love.' ... Thus, I was taught that Love was our Lord's meaning. (Chapter 86)

Sometimes, as Martin Luther King Jr discovered, it is in moments of the deepest pain or sorrow or helplessness that a wave of hope and light breaks into our darkness. Then we experience grace, God's merciful love, and everything is transformed.

Julian is totally in the mainstream of church tradition when she sees Christianity as an incarnational, 'enfleshed' way of life. For her, the Passion of Jesus is meant to impinge upon our senses, to be 'seen', to be gazed at contemplatively. This is what the devotion of the Stations of the Cross invites us to do: to look on

Jesus as he makes his sorrowful journey to Calvary. As we do so, we become aware that our pain, our sufferings, are caught up in his. We learn that we do not suffer alone, we suffer with him and he with us. Sometimes, in retrospect, we may even find, as Julian did, that the hardest times in life have brought the deepest joy. It is the presence of the Holy Spirit that brings this joy, keeps hope alive in us when nothing seems right, gives us the courage to keep going when everything is painful and difficult.

Although in her book Julian does not describe a prolonged 'dark night' experience, but speaks rather of the spiritual ups and downs that are common to everyone, it is clear that her mystical visions did not free her from pain and suffering. Her temperament may have been naturally sanguine and hopeful, but her awareness of evil and her struggle with temptation never left her. There were times, she tells us, when her battle with the spirit of evil (in the language of her time, she calls evil 'the fiend' and is acutely aware of its power) kept her busy throughout the night. Yet her mysticism is one of joyful trust, and a robust spirit of hope runs right through her book, *Showing of Love*. Towards the end of the book, there is one short quotation in particular that seems to bring together both her realistic stance before the problem of evil and her constant hopefulness. It comes in what Julian calls 'a restful showing ... and this was a singular joy and bliss', and she says that the words she heard on that day brought her 'true comfort':

He [our good Lord] said not, 'You shall not be tempested [tempted], you shall not be travailed [troubled], you shall not be diseased [made uneasy],' but he said, 'You shall not be overcome.' God wills that we should take heed at these words, and that we be ever mighty in secure trust in weal and woe, for he loves and likes us. And so, he wills that we love and like him, and mightily trust in him. And all shall be well. (Chapter 68)

Goodness, she had learned, is always stronger than evil.

In her book, as we have seen, Julian wrestles with the problem of evil and suffering. She experiences the tension between her awareness of God's love and her personal knowledge of pain and sinfulness in the world. Does not this tension contradict God's assurance that 'All shall be well'? Ann Lewin, in her poem, 'Dark Moments', enters into the deep well of

Julian's hope, a hope that is strong even in the midst of fear. She suggests that the comfort of the words 'All shall be well' comes at a cost: the cost of hoping against hope, the cost of an unshakeable trust in God's providential love.

'All shall be well ...'

She must have said that
sometimes through gritted teeth.
Surely she knew the moments
when fear gnaws at trust,
the future loses shape.

The courage that says
all shall be well
doesn't mean feeling no fear,
but facing it, trusting
God will not let go.

All shall be well
doesn't deny present experience
but roots it deep
in the faithfulness of God,
whose will and gift is life.

Sometimes, overtly 'religious' or 'spiritual' advice, offered in good faith to those who are suffering, can seem impossibly simplistic: 'Say your prayers and everything will work out for the best!' But we do not and truly cannot understand suffering; the mystery of God as found in human misery simply cannot be fathomed. Ann Lewin's poem suggests that Julian was well aware of this, but she believes we can learn to endure suffering and other distressing experiences by tuning in to the nearness of God. Julian's message is: God walks with us in our sinfulness and suffering in a relationship of love, and nothing, nothing at all, can separate us from that love. That is why, in the end, all shall be well. God's loving faithfulness leads Julian to hope in a destiny beyond death and suffering, and hope means waiting for God to break into our lives, bringing new life and transformation, bringing resurrection. She has an unwavering confidence that God walks with us in all that happens to us, and because of this, she knows in her heart that goodness is stronger than evil, and that perfect love overcomes death.

I recently came across a moving example of this indestructible hope in God's love, articulated in the song of a homeless man in London. The Yorkshire composer, Gavin Bryars, says he heard this song in 1971, when he was working with a friend on a film about people living on the streets in the Elephant and Castle/Waterloo area of south London. He says that in the course of being filmed, some of the people they interviewed 'broke into drunken song – sometimes bits of opera, sometimes sentimental ballads – and one, who in fact did not drink, sang a religious song, "Jesus' Blood Never Failed Me Yet"'. Bryars was very struck by this song, and recorded it. When he played the recording at home, he found that the man's singing was in tune with his piano, so he spontaneously improvised a simple accompaniment. Later, he was doing some further work on this song in the recording studio, and one day, quite by chance, a number of people happened to hear it. Some were so deeply moved that they sat there in silence, listening and quietly weeping. It was a totally unprompted response and it convinced Bryars of the emotional power of the voice and the music. He went on to compose what he called 'a simple, though gradually evolving, orchestral accompaniment that respected the homeless man's nobility and simple faith'. He says that although the old man died before he could hear what had been done with his singing, 'the piece remains as an eloquent, but understated testimony to his spirit and optimism'.

The old man's message was unambiguous: God loves him, God has watched over him all his life and always will:

> Jesus' blood never failed me yet
> Never failed me yet
> Jesus' blood never failed me yet
> This one thing I know
> That He loves me so
> Jesus' blood won't fail me yet
> won't fail me yet
> won't fail me yet
> Jesus' blood never failed me yet
> Never failed me yet
> Jesus' blood never failed me yet
> This one thing I know
> That He loves me so

This is a song of hope, a song about the nearness of God as experienced in the bleak life of a destitute man who for many years had been sleeping rough on the streets of London. Instead of being crushed and embittered by life, he seems to have been able to retain his peace and serenity in the midst of human failure and pain. It is hope that stretches the limits of what is possible, hope that encourages us to believe that goodness is indeed stronger than evil, that love is stronger than hate, that light is stronger than darkness.

The story of this old man, nameless and homeless, demonstrates with touching simplicity the truth of Shakespeare's words: 'The miserable have no other medicine but only hope.' The more desperate the situation, the stronger the hope ... In Jesus, this man discovered a friend who suffered with him, who became vulnerable with him, who walked with him on his journey through life. Poor in spirit and poor in reality, he knew his need of God, and his trust in God's goodness was wholehearted and unconditional. His Christian faith and hope made him ready to bear the cross of the present, and drew him into a life of love. This old man may never have heard of Julian of Norwich, but the words of his song, sung with such sincerity, are in complete accord with hers: Love is God's meaning. The melody of his song was hope, and its rhythm was love.

In the spirit of that song, I cannot think of a better way to end this chapter than to quote from Bishop Tom Wright, who believes that hope is an absolutely crucial ingredient of the Christian message. In his book, *Surprised by Hope*, he writes:

> To hope for a better future in this world – for the poor, the lonely and distressed, for the abused, the paranoid, the downtrodden and despairing, and in fact for the whole wide, wonderful and wounded world – is not something else, something extra, something tacked on to 'the gospel' as an afterthought – it is a central, essential, vital and life-giving part of it.[3]

And the source of this hope is God's nearness in the whole of life.

Hope comes to birth in our world each time we hunger and thirst for what is right, each time we resist the impulse towards racism, marginalization and exclusion, each time we welcome the stranger, and stretch out a hand to help someone in need. Karl Rahner, SJ, puts it this way:

> Have we ever kept quiet, even though we wanted to defend ourselves, when we had been unfairly treated? Have we ever forgiven someone even though we got no thanks for it and our silent

forgiveness was taken for granted? ... Have we ever sacrificed something without receiving any thanks or recognition for it, and even without a feeling of inner satisfaction? Have we ever been absolutely lonely? Have we ever decided on some course of action purely by the innermost judgment of our conscience, deep down where one can no longer tell or explain it to anyone, where one is quite alone and knows that one is taking a decision which no one else can take in one's place and for which one will have to answer for all eternity?[4]

If we do any or all of these things, we fan a spark of hope into a living flame of love, and we mirror the God who makes goodness come out of evil.

FOR PERSONAL REFLECTION OR GROUP DISCUSSION

1 How do you respond to Chris Chivers' account of the 'Truth and Reconciliation' hearing that took place in Guguletu, South Africa, in 1996?

2 Why do you think the people who heard the old man's song, recorded by Gavin Bryars, were so moved by it?

3 Martin Luther King Jr's words of near-despair are honest and direct. Have you ever experienced a time of darkness in your own life when a small spark of hope gave you the strength to continue?

FURTHER SUGGESTIONS

1 Re-read Ann Lewin's poem about Julian of Norwich. How do you feel about this portrayal of a woman of hope?

2 Depictions of the 14 traditional 'Stations' of the Cross are found in all Roman Catholic churches. They are an encouragement to respond to these words of scripture: 'All you who pass this way, look and see: is there any sorrow like the sorrow that afflicts me?' (Lamentations 1.12). Go into a nearby church where you know you will find these pictures, and take a few moments to 'pass this way', saying a short prayer at each 'Station'.

Listen to a recording of Pergolesi's *Stabat Mater*. The composer, who died at the age of 26, said that this music was inspired by the tenth Station of the Cross: the death of Jesus, usually depicted showing Mary, grieving at the foot of the cross. If you prefer more modern music, you may like to listen to James MacMillan's masterpiece, *Stabat Mater*, composed in 2016.

3

HOPE AND COURAGE

'Take courage, all you people of the land, says the Lord, for I am with you, according to the promise I made you when you came out of Egypt. My spirit abides among you; do not be afraid.'

Haggai 2.4, 5

'Hope has two beautiful daughters,' said St Augustine; 'their names are Anger and Courage: anger at the way things are, and courage to see that they do not remain as they are.' These words express the natural relationship between hope, anger and courage, for in practice, the three are inseparable. Augustine calls both of hope's daughters beautiful, anger as well as courage, for this is honourable anger, the non-acceptance of an intolerable situation. Hope, he seems to say, is rightly angered by the wrongs and wounds of our broken world; it inspires courage to take steps to 'repair' what is broken, to take care of creation, to bind up its wounds. As I write this, I am reminded of a television interview I saw on the day Prince William launched the Earthshot project in October 2020. When he spoke of his desire to harness urgency with optimism, his words seemed to echo Augustine's. He said it was his hope that, through this 10-year global project, we humans will discover new ways to protect and restore the natural world. Spurred on by 'anger', by deep concern at the damage we have inflicted on the environment, often unknowingly, William had the courage to confront this critical problem, and to take action. Here Hope and her two beautiful daughters unite, inviting us to participate in the urgent task of attempting to rescue our fragile planet and to enrich its future.

Hope gives courage, and courage nourishes hope. Without hope, we could, and perhaps often would, take the easy way out and settle for leaving things as they are, even when we are rightly 'angry' about them and know that change is needed; without courage, our hopes for that change would never be realized. Without hope, we would be unable to see the light shining in the darkness; without courage, we wouldn't dare to follow the light. When the past and the present weigh heavily upon us, hope glimpses a more promising future, and it is courage that urges us to strain forward to what lies ahead. So it is that hope and courage are both needed on the human journey; without both, many important endeavours would never be undertaken, many difficult but critical tasks would never be accomplished. Hope and courage are also needed on the journey of Lent, as we walk in the footsteps of Jesus, accompanying him in his suffering and death and walking with him towards the new life of Easter. In a sense, hope is a balancing of impatience and patience, of reflection and action, of caution and haste, and it includes being open to both anguish and joy.

What is it, this hope that we cling to against all the odds? It is the conviction that, under God, things will get better, and we cling to it because we cannot help ourselves. Hope seems to be innate in us, rooted in a universal human longing for change – not change for its own sake, but transformation. Hope touches every aspect of our lives, trivial and significant, personal and communal, and it is creative and imaginative. Although often tentative and prone to disappointment, it is courageous, ready to step into the unknown, to face the unknowable. Hope is an affirmation of the future:

grounded in the past, conscious of the brokenness of the present, it nurtures the seedlings of future fruitfulness. Even in everyday language, when we say the word or write it, hope has a future orientation, and this is reflected in our grammar. 'Hope', used as a verb, is followed by the future tense, and the word has its own vocabulary – change, possibility, transformation, the new, the unprecedented, the better ... Our hope is for a future good both in our personal lives and in the world in which we live. But according to Rowan Williams, 'hope is not simply confidence in the future; it is confidence that past, present and future are held in one relationship'.

Hope is a passion for the possible, yet because it often alternates with fear that what it longs for will not come about, we need courage as well as hope. Animated by hope, courage helps us to begin again when we feel lost or bewildered, to face the ruins of the past and to commit ourselves to building a new future while accepting the uncertainties of the present. Hope is realistic; it recognizes that life, or our experience of it, is neither utterly bad nor perfect, and at the same time it imagines, visualizes, what does not yet exist, so it is always looking for new possibilities. From some of the tragic, devastating or unpleasant realities of today, many of them inherited from yesterday, hope points to the dreams of tomorrow. Hope is a starting point, a basis for action; anger pushes us forward, urging us to face the difficulties, while courage seeks new ways of dealing with them. Through hope, anger and courage, by making changes in what we do and the way we live, we in some sense anticipate a future that is hidden from us. Jürgen Moltmann says it beautifully: 'By changing ourselves and the circumstances around us, by anticipating the future God, we emigrate out of the past into the future.'

How we long for that hidden future to announce itself, and soon! Yet the coming of God's reign, when we believe all things will reach their fulfilment in love, goodness and truth, often seems very distant, or to be contradicted by the present as we know and experience it. Although it is true that today many of us are making more conscious and more concerted efforts to promote peace and justice, and to walk on the earth – God's earth and our common home – with greater sensitivity, more responsibly aware of our relationship with the natural world that nurtures and sustains us, we still have far to go. And the climate emergency is only one of the many deeply disturbing issues in the world of our time. If what St Augustine calls 'anger at the way things are' is to lead to a serious attempt to improve the situation, we need an active hope, and the courage to search for communal solutions to our global problems.

There is hope for a better world, but it is in our power to snuff out that hope by our pessimism or lack of courage, or by allowing the anger we feel to paralyse us. On the other hand, we can fan hope into a flame by cultivating a more positive approach to life, and by looking for ways to encourage one another to do this. Especially when present sufferings seem to be overwhelming, hope helps us to be open to hearing both the cry of anger and the call to courage. Hope and courage can illumine the dark lands of despair, and it is good to remember that we have within us an inborn capacity for hopefulness. This does not mean suppressing our anger, or closing our eyes to the terrible things we hear about or experience personally, but it does mean balancing them against an awareness of the many often unnoticed and unrecorded hopeful things that happen around us every day, if we have eyes to see and ears to hear.

Anne Frank, in a particularly moving passage in her diary of 1944, has a similar message. Her words undramatically demonstrate that to have hope is to live somewhere between anger at the way things are and an ardent longing for them to get better:

> The difficulty in these times is that ideals, dreams and cherished hopes rise within us, only to meet the horrible truth and be shattered. It's really a wonder that I haven't dropped all my ideals, because they seem so absurd and impossible to carry out. Yet I keep them, because, in spite of everything, I still believe that people are really good at heart. I simply can't build up my hopes on a foundation consisting of confusion, misery and death. I see a world gradually being turned into a wilderness, I hear ever-approaching thunder, which will destroy us too; I can see the suffering of millions. And yet, if I look up into the heavens, I think it will all come right, that this cruelty too will end and that peace and tranquillity will return again.

Coming from the pen of a vulnerable 15-year-old girl, these words seem to gather up the fragments of a crushed community, yet the melody of hope, gentle but unmistakable, rings through them. In her awareness of what was happening all around her, Anne expresses her anger at what she calls 'the horrible truth'. But in the silence of her heart, she knows that there is more to this life than the gloom that encircles her. In these lines, she comes across as a kind of embodiment of hope, facing into despair and disaster without losing her peace of soul, and clinging courageously to the mystery of hope.

Hope implies not only anger and courage but wisdom too and patience; it includes accepting and learning to live with the things we cannot change, especially when those things are deeply disappointing or upsetting. It means living without losing heart in the face of inevitable frustrations or looming desperation. Hope is alive to the dreams of tomorrow but knows that those dreams are clothed in the reality of today. It is encouraging yet pragmatic, inspiring yet realistic: 'hopes and anticipations of the future are not a transfiguring glow superimposed on a darkened existence, but realistic ways of perceiving the scope of our real possibilities'.[2] Instinctively, many people seem to cling to hope in times of suffering, as Anne Frank did, seeking meaning, especially when life is challenging and chaotic, as it was for her. To live in hope stretches the limits of what is possible and influences the unfolding of the future. If it is true that the here and now contains a certain dynamism towards a more fulfilling future, then that dynamism is hope. Hope, in the words of Helen Keller, 'sees the invisible, feels the intangible, and achieves the impossible'. And hope's companion, courage, is, according to Goethe, a quality without which a human being would be better off never having been born.

When we walk on the edges of life and death, when we're angry, downcast or depressed, fearful or anxious, hope can open us to God's loving presence at the heart of life, point to a path that will lead to consolation, if we have the courage to take it. Hope is not an evasion of human realities; it doesn't mean looking the other way or failing to deal with obvious difficulties by side-stepping them. Rather, it helps us to confront problems and challenges by putting us in touch with eternal realities. Hope moves us beyond purely logical reasoning, which can lead into the bleak territory of desperation; it enables us to keep our eyes open in the dark, and awakens in us the capacity to imagine and prepare for a different future. When, in Paul's words, our 'inward eyes' are illumined, we can see more clearly the hope to which God is calling us. St Thérèse of Lisieux, the young French Carmelite nun who died in 1897 at the age of 24, clearly saw the divine dimension of hope. She once wrote: 'My hopes touch upon the infinite.' How right she was. All true hope touches upon the infinite: it gives us the courage to look forward to a transformation that only God can give. Pope Francis, in his recent encyclical, *Fratelli tutti*,[3] beautifully expresses something of the profound meaning of hope and links it with courage: 'Hope speaks to us of a thirst, an aspiration, a longing for a life of fulfilment, a desire to achieve great things, things that fill our heart and lift our spirit to lofty realities like truth, goodness and beauty, justice and love ... Hope is bold ...'

In his book about the Easter Gospel, Archbishop Rowan Williams says that resurrection is only discovered through repentance or conversion ('metanoia'), which he sees as 'the refusal to accept that lostness is the final human truth'. Turning to God, refusing to wander in the dark without God, is, I believe, a perfect way to describe hope, for it is hope that shapes our intention to walk through the sombre places of our lives, not alone, but in God's presence. In his book, Williams recounts a deeply moving story about a teenager who took his own life during the Troubles in Northern Ireland. It is a story that illustrates, he says, 'a kind of unspoken,

un-formulable hope ... barely recognizable as hope'.
Here are his words:

> A mother noticed her teenage son was in
> obvious distress and fear; when questioned, he
> admitted that he was involved with a (Protestant)
> paramilitary group, which had ordered him to
> perform a killing locally, or else face 'execution'
> himself. The mother was able to say, eventually,
> that being killed was preferable to killing; that
> night her son hanged himself.[4]

Commenting on this tragic suicide, Williams calls it a

> converted act ... a statement that the human
> world is not-at-home, is estranged, 'improper',
> when it closes itself up in threats and murder. And
> the one who has thus 'turned' in refusal from a
> trapped world may indeed be turning to hear his
> or her name spoken by the Lord.

Hurt is terribly disturbing; when that sorrowing
mother, having listened to her son's pain, later found
he had taken his own life, she would have felt utterly
crushed and broken. One can only hope and pray that,

with the passing of time, in the grief of her loss and the anguish of her sense of guilt, she might have found comfort in the thought that God does not turn away from those who are trapped or misguided. When the past, dark and shameful as it may appear to be, is faced in God's loving presence, it is recovered in hope.

Sometimes, hope, the second of those virtues that we call 'theological', tends to be overlooked, submerged, hidden as it were between faith and love. Yet St Paul, who calls love 'the greatest of the three', and whose hymn to love is universally admired and often quoted by Christians and non-Christians alike, has no intention of ignoring hope. He gives it his full attention, naming it 35 times in his letters, and underlining its central importance for the journey of faith. By faith, we become friends of God, believing in his promises, sustained by his word. In a sense, faith, when it looks to the future, becomes hope, which is poured into our hearts by the Holy Spirit. And faith and hope always lead to love, the culmination and crown of the Christian life, for love never comes to an end. Hope, for Paul, is a clear sign of God's nearness, it is 'a fragrance of the divinity' (2 Corinthians 2.14). It is not deceptive, not a mirage, not merely a comforting illusion; nor is it a kind of opium that simply deadens the pain of present miseries. Instead, like the word of God, it is alive and active. It gives us the inner strength to face the trials and ordeals of life, and, if we cannot change them, to endure them with peace of soul, because we believe that our lives are in God's hands. Hope, for Paul, brings peace and joy: 'Rejoice in hope, be patient in suffering, persevere in prayer' he says in the letter to the Romans (12.12). God is the source of our hope, and 'in hope we were saved' (8.24).

Hope – that amazing energy that challenges and inspires us to keep going in difficult times – is a gift that could only come from God. Charles Péguy's poem about hope[5] echoes the sense of mystery associated with this virtue: our conviction that things will get better, in spite of some of the dreadful situations we all have to face, is impossible to understand or explain. In the opening lines of this poem, which is written in free verse, we hear the voice of God saying that faith doesn't surprise him in the least – our eyes have only to look, and we will be carried effortlessly into the realm of faith. Is not God's presence revealed in the universe? Is not the divine visible on the face of the earth, on the face of the waters, in the movement of the stars, in the wind that blows over land and sea, in mountains and valleys and forests and fields, in peoples and nations, in men and women? Do we not see God, above all, in children – in their innocent gaze, in the purity of their voices? In order not to believe, not to have faith, we would have to do violence to ourselves, we would have to cover our eyes and block our ears. Charity, too, is unsurprising, says God in Péguy's poem. After all, if we are to love those close to us, we cannot ignore or avoid charity. And we are surrounded by so many unfortunates, so many desolate, unhappy, hurting people, that we would need to have hearts of stone not to respond to them, our brothers and sisters, in their need. How could we not desire to share our bread with those who are hungry?

Yes, according to Péguy, God sees faith and charity as perfectly straightforward; they are easily understandable. It is hope that God finds astounding – a mystery indeed! That we see all that is happening around us today and still believe that tomorrow will be better,[6] that, says God, is really astonishing, given that the temptation to lose hope constantly hovers over us. Péguy's hope is not optimism, when we just shrug our shoulders and 'hope for the best'. He presents hope as at once natural and supernatural, as time-bound and eternal, as earthly and spiritual, as mortal and immortal, human and divine. In the darkness that surrounds us, hope may be like a flickering candle-flame, diminutive, feeble, but, he says, that flame cannot be extinguished, even by the breath of death itself. Péguy personifies Hope, as he does Faith and Charity; he sees them as three sisters, walking together along the rough, stony road that leads to salvation. As they walk, Faith is on one side, Charity on the other, while in the middle is little Hope, almost hidden in the skirts of her two older siblings.

The poet cannot resist some vivid images. Faith is like a cathedral, built on sturdy foundations, solid, ancient, venerable, lasting for centuries. She is a spouse, steadfast and upright, a faithful wife. Her demeanour is marked, as is fitting for such an important virtue, by the gravitas and wisdom of an older woman. Charity, on the other hand, is like a hospital, an alms-house, and there she gathers up all the miseries of the world, there she welcomes the wounded, the sick, the sorrowful, the unwanted. She is a mother, full of heart, compassionate, kind and gentle. Her eyes shine with loving concern, her hands are outstretched to help all those in need. She cannot do otherwise. But what of Hope? Péguy presents Hope as a child, a little girl, innocent, trusting, defenceless. He describes her as '*une petite fille de rien du tout*', and this little bit of nothing turns out to be the perfect metaphor for Hope. Children are amazingly compassionate: they shed tears when they see anyone who is unhappy, they weep over a hurt animal or a broken toy. They love to play, they carry no heavy burdens, and hope seems to come naturally to them. In the poem, Hope is a child who skips along the road of life between her two older sisters, carefree and joyful, and no one takes much notice of her. Every night she goes to bed, sleeps really well, and every morning she gets up refreshed and renewed.

Péguy's Hope brings faith and love into the orbit of ordinary human living. She knows it is not easy, or even possible, for us to believe in God unceasingly and without ever doubting; she knows too that it is impossible for us always to love everyone, especially people we do not like or who do us harm. Vulnerable but invincible, Hope sensitizes us to notice the tiny glimmers of light in the thick darkness that so often envelops us; she reminds us that if our faith weakens and we lose sight of God on life's journey, we can always rediscover his presence and walk with him again. As for charity, Hope reveals that mutuality is its true fulfilment. For charity is not just giving, giving, giving to those in need; it is also receiving from them, valuing what they offer, and it is Hope that prompts this recognition of the importance of a reciprocal exchange of gifts. Hope gives us the spiritual energy to endure hardship, to live with a measure of serenity even in the face of major complications and difficulties. It helps us to see things from a different perspective, from God's perspective, and God seeks to liberate, to bring life.

Published in 1911, Péguy wrote his poem about hope when the shadows of the First World War were gathering over Europe (a war in which – in 1914, at the age of 41 – he was to die, fighting, as he believed, for general disarmament) in an atmosphere of increasing political and economic tension. Without philosophizing, without moralizing, uttering no warnings, offering no lightweight prescriptions, he proposes a radical therapy for the world of his time: hope. Like the biblical prophets, he discerns God's presence in concrete human experiences. For him, hope flows from his reading of creation, where God speaks, transforming anguish into compassion, failure into creative abandonment, distress into tenderness, desperation into confidence. Péguy is God's scribe, and God's message is hope, surely a message that, more than a century later, we need to hear, loud and clear, today, in our confused, polluted, degraded, coronavirus-infected world.

In his encyclical letter of 2007, *Spe salvi* ('Saved by Hope'), Pope Benedict XVI wrote: 'the one who has hope has been granted the gift of new life'. Two men who received this gift were Brian Keenan, a teacher, and John McCarthy, a BBC journalist. Both these men were abducted as hostages in Beirut in 1986 by Islamist Jihadi terrorists, and spent five years in captivity. They did not regard themselves as practising Christians, but in an indefinable way 'God' became real for them during that time. In his book, *An Evil Cradling*, Brian reveals that faith and hope helped both men to survive their terrifying ordeal. He says that they prayed unashamedly, and through their conversations during those years of enforced confinement, they forged a strong bond that helped them to survive. Despair constantly beckoned them, and they had no idea if or when they would ever be released; but it seems that their acceptance of their joint experience generated hope in the two men, and their companionship gave them the courage to keep going. They felt they were in God's hands.

In the same encyclical, Benedict says that if we have hope, the present is touched by a future reality not yet visible in the external world, and that through hope we carry within us a certain perception of this reality. Does taking part in the celebration of Eucharist affirm that touch, illuminate that perception? In spite of all we are told (and know to be true) about the decline of faith and churchgoing in our time, it seems that the Christian practice of beginning the day with this sacred ritual has not completely disappeared. There are still some people who wish to attend daily Eucharist, especially during Lent. In doing so, it may be that they seek to experience God's touch in their lives, in their joys and sorrows and day-to-day struggles. We live in a time of crisis on many fronts, and perhaps we are aware that our faith has weakened, so we count on God's touch to animate us as we make our Lenten journey in the hope of the new life of Easter.

In Paris, where I spent three years recently, I have a clear memory of attending daily Mass during the season of Lent in the weekday chapel of our local church. For six weeks, at 7.30, often on cold, grey, rainy mornings, I would join 15 or 20 people, men and women of different ages and backgrounds, who had gathered there – a pattern no doubt repeated in churches and chapels all over the world. Each morning we got up a bit earlier than we strictly needed to, and denied ourselves the pleasure of really savouring that first cup of coffee of the day. Why did we do this? Was it worth the effort? What were we hoping for? I suspect that those people, like myself, were seeking God's blessing at the start of the day. The early service usually lasted less than half an hour – it was not rushed, but the priest did not delay; he knew that many of the members of that little congregation would be hurrying off to work very soon afterwards. The readings were made expeditiously, peace was shared, the bread and wine of communion given and received with due reverence. And then, after the final blessing, everyone quietly left, some stopping off in the local boulangerie to buy a baguette to eat on their way to work ...

Many years ago, when I was a young teacher in Paisley, a 13-year-old girl in one of my classes was knocked down by a car on her way home from school. In that part of Scotland, in mid-February, before the clocks go forward, it is already dusk by 4 o'clock, and perhaps Kathleen in her navy-blue school uniform was invisible to the driver of that car. Who knows? Although the accident happened in the centre of the town, those were the days before CCTV became mandatory and the driver was never traced – 'a classic hit and run incident', said the local newspaper. Kathleen was taken to hospital, but never recovered consciousness and died the following day. Her grieving parents told me she had attended Mass at the cathedral on her way to school that morning. It was a comfort to them to know this – that their beloved daughter had begun her day by placing in God's hands all that would happen to her. She did not know that it was to be the last day of her young life, but she did know that she wanted to offer it to God.

Kathleen lived at some distance from the school and had to catch an earlier train in order to take part in that Lenten Eucharist before the school day began. It seems that she, like the people in that church in Paris, wished to make this part of her daily routine during the season of Lent. In doing this, she, and they, were, I believe, seeking the touch of God. I am reminded of the words of the Bengali poet, Rabindranath Tagore:

I have come to thee to take thy touch before I begin my day.

Let thy eyes rest upon my eyes for a while.
Let me take to my work the assurance of thy
comradeship, my friend.

Here, of course, Tagore, who was a devout Hindu,
is not referring to daily attendance at the Eucharist,
but his words capture the spirit of this long-standing
Lenten practice and suggest why it should continue
to have an appeal for those who simply wish to take
their place in a community of believers and ask God
to walk with them in the events of the coming day.
The poet's tender words make it clear that he wished
to do the same.

When, in a spirit of hope, we open ourselves to the
touch of God in this way, we place in God's hands the
expected and unexpected happenings, the joys and
difficulties, we may encounter in the day ahead. So
this short time of prayer becomes a kind of 'morning
offering' of the things we will do, whether eagerly
anticipated, stoically accepted or mutely dreaded. As
we do this, we also lay before God the people who
will cross our path in the course of the day – those
we know and like and those we know and dislike,
as well as those we do not know or have never met
before. And if we feel helpless in the face of some

of the seemingly insurmountable problems in our personal lives and in our world, hope can spur us on, so that our helplessness does not paralyse us. In times of sadness and desolation, the touch of God awakens hope in us. Then we are less likely to be submerged by our anxieties and fears, less likely to miss the sudden glimpses of goodness and beauty, the flashes of inspiration that can come our way, even in the midst of inevitable tensions and disappointments. Lent without Easter is inconceivable, and hope is one of the leitmotifs of Lent. In our Lenten prayer and reflection, we become more deeply aware of God's saving touch not only in the death and resurrection of Jesus, but in our own lives and in the life of the world.

'More things are wrought by prayer than this world dreams of ...' said Tennyson, gracefully carrying us into the domain of transcendence. Yes, in a truly amazing way, prayer enables us to pass on to others the touch of God. John Ames, the elderly pastor in Marilynne Robinson's novel *Gilead*, took this for granted:

It was on the nights I didn't sleep at all and I didn't feel like reading that I'd walk through town at one or two o'clock. In the old days I could walk down every

single street, past every house, in about an hour. I'd
try to remember the people who lived in each one,
and whatever I knew about them, which was often
quite a lot ... And I'd pray for them. And I'd imagine
peace they didn't expect and couldn't account for
descending on their illness or their quarrelling or
their dreams. Then I'd go into the church and pray
some more and wait for daylight ...[7]

Ames here is bringing before God in prayer the
concerns and heartbreaks of the men and women of
the small American town where he lived. His trust in
God is strong, and his words convey a deep conviction
of the relevance, the 'rightness', of this silent but
pastoral act. He has no doubts: he is passing on the
touch of God.

And where does the touch of God fit into our
preconceived ideas of Lent? If you are continuing to
read this book, you probably have a desire to mark
this liturgical season in some way, and to prepare for
the celebration of Easter. But what does Lent mean? Is
it simply six long weeks, Sundays excepted, without
alcohol (or with less), without cigarettes (or with
fewer), without meat (on Fridays, at least), without
television or whatever superfluities we decide to give

up this year? If so, in the last analysis, it will surely have little appeal, and we'll embark on it unenthusiastically to say the least, dreading rather than embracing it. If instead we see Lent as an opportunity to reflect on how we could be more open to the touch of God in our lives, then, when Easter comes, perhaps we would see stones rolled away and new possibilities revealed.

All the days of Lent are oriented towards the good news of the Resurrection, which is the core of our faith and the source of our hope. Pope Francis, in his little book, *The Joy of the Gospel*, has this to say: 'There are Christians whose lives seem like Lent without Easter ... I understand the grief of people who have to endure great suffering, yet slowly but surely we have to let the joy of faith revive as a quiet yet firm trust, even amid the greatest distress.' Francis goes on to quote from the Book of Lamentations: '[M]y soul is bereft of peace; I have forgotten what happiness is ... But this I call to mind, and therefore I have hope: the steadfast love of the Lord never ceases, his mercies never come to an end; they are new every morning' (3:17, 21–23). This is the message of Lent, its purpose and its gift: to look towards the resurrection of Jesus with hope and courage, and resurrection, new life, is discovered by responding to the touch of God in our lives. We are not only the recipients but also the transmitters of hope. Passing on God's touch to the people we meet, especially those who 'have forgotten what happiness is', is to spread the good news of God's loving presence among us, especially when they or we meet with pain and disappointment. To do that is the mission of all Christians, and it is hope that gives us the spiritual energy to carry out this mission.

FOR REFLECTION OR GROUP DISCUSSION

1 How do you respond to the excerpt from Anne Frank's diary given in this chapter?

2 Why, in Péguy's poem, does God find hope so astonishing?

3 Have you ever had a conversation that gave you fresh hope when you were feeling really down?

FURTHER SUGGESTIONS

1 Bring to mind some hopeful things that you have read or heard about so far this Lent. Make a note of them, and share them with a friend in a letter or email.

2 Re-read the passage about John Ames. Do you
   see the pastor's prayers for his people as an act
   of hope?

3 Find two small stones, and keep them in your
   pocket during Lent – a reminder of some things
   in your life (grudges, misunderstandings,
   resentments) that would need to be 'rolled
   away' if new possibilities are to be revealed.
   Roll them away when Easter comes ...

4

SIGNS AND SYMBOLS

'Symbols are powerful because they are the visible signs of invisible realities.'

St Augustine

As we try to engage with Lent, reflecting on our faith, we become more keenly aware not only of our personal desires and fears, struggles and temptations, but of the immense problems of the globalized civilization in which we live. Few of us would deny that, faced with that reality, hope is vital. In his letter to the Romans, St Paul wrote, 'Who hopes for what is seen? But if we hope for what we do not see, we wait for it with patience' (8.24, 25). His words are eminently true; but we are human, and if we are to become aware of the invisible realities that Augustine speaks of in the above quotation, we need signs, perceptible indications of their presence, to keep our hope alive. Signs and symbols remind us of God's nearness, and if we are alert and open to them, they help to keep us on track through the weeks of Lent so that we can move more confidently towards Easter. They point to gifts and possibilities in people, in situations and experiences, and through them, we become more aware of what the world is, of the heights and depths of existence, and of God's loving presence in all that happens to us.

I sometimes feel our Western society has a bias towards noise and haste, and as a result, quietness does not appear to be greatly valued. Many people seem to hold the view that to be alive in a fully human sense is to be always busy, always on the go, and they set themselves to accomplish an exhausting variety of tasks, day after day. Yet it has to be said that most of us will be unable to find God amid constant clamour and activity, if we have not first found him in inwardness and stillness. According to the great twentieth-century Jewish theologian and philosopher, Abraham Heschel, hope is a 'seed of eternity planted in the soul', and seeds of eternity emerge little by little ... Hope is born in the readiness to wait on God, to wait patiently for what we long for, believing that God has our best interests at heart. Hope has its own dynamism, but I think it would be true to say that it does not usually manifest itself in compulsive busyness, noise, hustle and bustle. With Covid-19, we have been and are inhabiting a strange new world, and certainly there are not many obvious benefits to be found in it. However, perhaps one bonus is that we are being led into a more thoughtful mode, and as we find ourselves obliged to confront inevitable suffering, hardship and uncertainty, the instinct of hope comes into its own.

Ever since the outbreak of this devastating virus, there have been few speeches, reports and articles, political or other, that do not encourage, overtly or obliquely, a spirit of hopefulness. And that hopefulness springs not simply from confidence in the NHS or in sophisticated vaccines and other medical remedies, though of course these are essential; rather surprisingly, given the apparently faithless times in which we live, it seems to come from a sense of the nearness of God. What is happening in our world shapes our faith, strengthens it, and all around us, if we are on the alert, we will hear stories, witness human actions, that give expression to hope and courage. I believe these things are signs that God is with us, accompanying us, working in us and through us during these difficult times. In September

2020, when anxiety about the second wave of the coronavirus was mounting in Britain, the First Minister of Scotland, Nicola Sturgeon, said this: 'Let's keep going, try to keep smiling, keep hoping and keep looking out for each other. Be strong, be kind and let's continue to act out of love and solidarity.' In the same week, walking on the Thames Path near Limehouse in east London, I heard two people talking quietly behind me. As they passed, one of them said, 'She's in a really bad way, poor thing – my brother said she's been on a ventilator for three weeks.' 'Yes,' said his companion, a woman. 'We must pray really hard for her and for the whole family; they're worried sick.' The young couple walked on, so I heard no more of this conversation, but I was touched by the sincerity of their voices, struck by this audible sign of their faith. Then, in October 2020, during the Santander Triathlon, Diego Méntriga noticed that his co-runner, James Teagle, had, just metres from the finishing-line, taken a wrong turn. Believing that Teagle deserved to be the winner, he waited for him, sacrificing his own chance to take third place in the race. The report of this action spread throughout the globe in seconds – a powerful sign of hope in the highly competitive world of sport.

And other hopeful signs have not been lacking. It has been widely reported that in the course of the varying degrees of lockdown, many people felt they had developed a greater appreciation of nature. Some said this had prompted them to question their personal lifestyle, and they now want to be more proactive in our common task of protecting and caring for our fragile planet. Many also became aware that, with far fewer aeroplanes in the air above us and fewer vehicles on our roads, pollution had lessened considerably. In the cleaner air, some were doing more walking or cycling and found they were enjoying better health as a consequence. It is also undeniable that this worrying time has produced clear signs of a deep human solidarity, as thousands of volunteers gave time and energy to delivering food and other essentials to people with limited mobility, and cared for the sick and the housebound. I noticed too that we seemed to greet strangers more readily than we used to: in my part of London, as we passed one another in the street, waited at a supermarket checkout or at a bus stop, quite a bit of nodding and smiling went on – far more than before. It seems that our attitude has begun to change, and there were and are signs to prove it.

The sheer force of signs and symbols, compared with plain, unadorned verbal statements, is palpable. God is invisible, but everywhere there are visible signs of the divine presence. The Psalmist tells us that although 'No speech, no word, no voice is heard ...' yet 'the heavens proclaim the glory of God' (19.3, 1). The universe itself speaks to us through signs and symbols: the changing of the seasons, darkness and light, the skies and the stars, fields and forests and mountains, winding rivers, the wind in the trees, the restless sea. In this chapter, we are going to give some attention to the signs and symbols of hope that are part of the Christian journey of faith. It is fitting for us to do this in the season of Lent, which is itself symbolic, recalling as it does the 40 days that Jesus spent in the wilderness. He had just been baptized by John, and had been assured of his Father's love: 'This is my Son, the beloved, with whom I am well pleased' (Matthew 3.17). Strengthened by these words, Jesus was able to prepare himself for his forthcoming ministry by fasting and praying. It was clearly a testing time for him, but through it all, his trust in God enabled him to endure the rigours of abstaining from food and to resist the temptations of Satan. Matthew's account of this episode in Jesus' life ends with a sign of God's provident care for his Son: he tells us that 'angels came and waited on him' (4.11).

Signs and symbols are sometimes called the language of the soul, the language of dreams and visions and longings, and they are found in all human communities, and in every sphere, secular and religious. They permit us to convey the meaning of abstract ideas and spiritual concepts non-verbally as well as verbally, and they have always played a significant role in both religion and culture. They appeal to the senses and emotions and are thought to carry an 'inner' meaning, a spiritual meaning. They offer us a way to 'interpret' the holy, the eternal, to throw some light on things beyond our understanding, to pass from the known to the unknown. Signs and symbols take many forms: smiles, tears, sounds, silence, music, gestures, actions, objects, colours, words, dreams and visual images. And any or all of these things may lend themselves to the communication of the invisible, inaudible, intangible, inexpressible reality that is hope.

In our everyday lives, most of the signs we see and hear around us are concrete, with unambiguous meanings. Hand signals, arrows, hazard lights, traffic lights, badges, graphics, logos, police sirens, ambulance sirens, door bells, morse code, words like 'stop' and 'no entry' – all these signs aim to inform, warn or instruct. Also, in communicating with other people, we sometimes use simple physical gestures, like crossed fingers, nodding or shaking the head, finger to the lips, or 'thumbs up'. Everyone knows what these signs mean – and most of them cross cultural boundaries. Symbols, however, represent something less easily definable, so their meaning is not only less precise but may also be multi-faceted. Symbols are signs, but signs with deeper, more complex meanings, and often the message they convey has meaning for a specific community. Their function is to point beyond the representation to a deeper reality. Symbols touch into our inner world, the world of the spirit.

Both signs and symbols are an integral part of the 'language' of religious faith, and in that context, they are invested with spiritual meaning and seen as indications of God's nearness. Religious signs and symbols help us to interpret existence in the light of faith, as we search for the deeper significance of universal human experiences like birth and growth, joy and sadness, suffering and death. They readily lend themselves to the expression of our instinctive tendency to hope for better things: when we find ourselves confronted by lies, evil and ugliness, we long for truth, goodness and beauty. In the religious sense, hope is the confident expectation of a future that God has promised. The reason for our confidence is beautifully expressed in a verse from the prophet Jeremiah, who speaks to the people on God's behalf: 'For surely I know the plans I have for you, plans for your welfare and not for harm, to give you a future with hope' (29.11).

Certain symbols of hope inherited from the Jewish-Christian tradition have come to enjoy a quasi-universal significance. One of the most famous, the rainbow, although mediated through the Hebrew scriptures, has pre-biblical origins, thought to be rooted in the ancient cultures of Mesopotamia. The rainbow, the classic symbol of hope, was perceived as evidence in the sky of God's promise that the earth would never again be destroyed by a natural disaster. Ever since the outbreak of the coronavirus pandemic, we have seen rainbows everywhere, large, small, hand-painted or computerized graphics. Children were encouraged to paint them, and they were stuck on windows and pinned to doors and gates, as once again that particular symbol came into its own, expressing hope for deliverance through its distinctive sequence of colours. The bright, multi-coloured rainbows of all those artists, young and old, were wordlessly telling us that although things may look bad for us during these dark days, there is hope for a different future. It looks as if we shall be living in the shadow of that virus for some time to come, and the rainbows of hope will not soon disappear ...

In Christianity, the most ancient and widely recognized symbol is of course the cross, which is also the major symbol of the season of Lent. The cross was hailed in a sixth-century Latin hymn as the 'only hope' of salvation. How could a cross, which outwardly signifies suffering, disgrace and humiliation, be seen as a symbol of hope? The Brazilian theologian and philosopher Leonardo Boff points to a fitting explanation:

The cross ... is the symbol of the rejection and violation of the sacred rights of God and the human being. It is the product of hatred. There are those who, committing themselves to the struggle to abolish the cross from the world, themselves have to suffer and bear the cross. The cross is imposed on them, inflicted on them, by the creators of crosses. But this cross is accepted. Not because a value is seen in it, but because there are those who burst asunder the logic of its violence by their love. To accept the cross is to be greater than the cross. To live thus is to be greater than death.[1]

Seen in this light, the Christian symbol of the cross reminds us that God brought victory out of defeat, life out of death, hope out of despair. Elizabeth Johnson echoes Boff's understanding of the cross as breaking the logic of violence: she says that 'Jesus' brutal death enacts the solidarity of the gracious and merciful God with all who die, and especially with victims of injustice, opening hope for resurrection amid the horror.'[2]

Another ancient symbol of hope is the anchor, whose use in Christianity appears to have originated in a verse from the letter to the Hebrews (6.18, 19), in which we are encouraged to grasp the hope held out to us. 'We have this hope, a sure and steadfast anchor of the soul.' The anchor here symbolizes the security of knowing God is near amid the gales and storms encountered on the sea of life. Just as the anchor keeps the ship and the mariners safe on a sea that is volatile and turbulent, so hope as the anchor of the soul gives stability to the Christian life and keeps us steadfast in times of trouble and distress. In the first century CE, during the period of the Roman persecutions, the early Christians used certain 'secret' signs to share their faith, and the anchor was one of these: its shape led them to see it as a cross 'in disguise'. Because of this, anchors, symbolizing hope in God's victory over evil and death, are engraved on many of the tombs in the Catacombs. When we feel within ourselves a restless longing for better things, and patience is needed, with hope as the soul's anchor, we reach out to God and find comfort: the darkness of the cross is lit by the light of resurrection.

The anchor did not disappear from Christian usage, and as time went on and there was no need for secrecy, the symbol of the cross was openly merged with the anchor, the two sometimes being fashioned into a crucifix. In the seventeenth century, George Herbert, in his poem, 'Hope', was no doubt inspired by those lines from Hebrews, and indeed it seems that both for him and for his contemporary, John Donne, the anchor was deeply symbolic. Herbert portrays Hope as a personification of Christ, who gives him first an anchor, and then an 'optick'. (The 'optick', or telescope, an important tool for astronomy, was invented during Herbert's lifetime.) For the poet, the telescope seems to symbolize our need to take on God's perspective, to take the long view, so that we can see the things of God with greater clarity. It is hope, he says, that enables us to do this. As we wait on God to reveal some glimmers of light in the darkness that surrounds us, the telescope is a symbol of the expanded vision that hope brings, and we need that today as much as ever.

There seems to be a deep human need to give expression to the divine in a tangible form, for God, though beyond all names and words, is not simply a disembodied abstraction. We are visual people, and we want to picture what God looks like, to 'see' God with our own eyes, to relate to God as persons do. Signs and symbols can and do put us in touch with that inward element of the physical life that the outward aspect hints at and suggests. It is not a question of seeing with our bodily eyes, but of an inner perceptiveness, insight, which we express through imagery and simile and metaphor, through signs and symbols. In our own lives, we know that earthly things, physical things, material realities, can lead us to a recognition of God's presence, and this experience is at the heart of our sacramental understanding of the world, for sacraments are sacred signs.

The majority of Christian denominations include two sacraments, Baptism and Eucharist, in their religious practice and acts of worship, while, in their rites, Anglican, Orthodox and Roman Catholic Christians observe seven. It must be said that sacraments, which outwardly signify God's unseen presence in the special moments of the journey of life, are not restricted to a particular number. God comes into our lives without any appointment and at any time, and each day, if we are not too preoccupied with other things, we will be aware of numerous signs of God's nearness. The message of poets and artists is perennial and its truth undeniable: in the midst of the banal reality of our lives, we can catch fleeting glimpses of the divine. Sudden flashes of inspiration, ephemeral 'sparkles' of God, sometimes come to us in the most unexpected situations. Glimpses and flashes and sparkles are by definition transient: they come and go. But although they do not stay with us, they can influence our thoughts and words and actions, and change our perceptions. If we take time to reflect, as we try to do in a special way in Lent, we realize that it really is true that, to use Elizabeth Barrett Browning's words from her book *Aurora Leigh*, 'Earth's crammed with heaven and every common bush afire with God'.

This awareness of God is crystallized in sacred signs and symbols, which can help us, as Francis Thompson said, to view the invisible, touch the intangible, know the unknowable, clutch what is inapprehensible. We live and move between two worlds, the material and the spiritual, and it is when these two worlds converge that we discern signs of God's presence, and experience the touch of God. The 'touch' of God is real; we know this instinctively because, usually in retrospect, we have 'felt' it.

In Holy Week 2019, I was living in Paris. For my little community of Faithful Companions of Jesus, that week began in Notre Dame Cathedral, as we listened to the last of the Lent Conferences, televised live on Palm Sunday. The very next day, 15 April, we were glued to the television all evening, watching in horror as sheets of flame consumed that beautiful cathedral. Along with the rest of Paris, indeed with the rest of the world, we felt utterly devastated, and experienced a sense of almost personal loss. The next morning, we heard that the fire crews had saved the familiar façade, the external walls and towers of the magnificent building, along with the stained-glass windows. But the slender, graceful spire, which had crowned the central section of the roof above the main nave, was almost completely incinerated in the extreme heat of the conflagration. Carved in oak and covered with lead, it had melted, and we saw what was left of it falling to the ground. Caught up in the drama of all that was happening before our eyes, our hope was shattered. Within days, it was rekindled when it was announced that a new spire would be created and placed on the roof once again. There it would resume its symbolic role: pointing to the heavens, reminding us of God's nearness.

It is true that when disaster strikes, as it struck that night in Paris, and as it had done in York in 1984, when the roof of the Minster caught fire, we can lose hope. When we call out to God from the depths of our distress and sense no immediate answer, sometimes we just want to give up. So, when we painfully realize that hope is drying up within us, when we find ourselves in a desperate situation and a positive outcome seems not only improbable but impossible, what can we do? How can we remain hopeful when the dream is dying, when our deepest longings have come to nothing? 'How could we sing a song of God on alien soil?' (Psalm 137.4). Is it worth trying to move on, to take the next step, when the road is long, when the journey seems never-ending, when there is no apparent solution to our problems? Vaclav Havel (the poet and playwright who was elected as the first president of the Czech Republic) has this to say:

> Hope ... is not the same as joy that things are going well, or willingness to invest in enterprises that are obviously headed for early success, but rather an ability to work for something because it is good, not just because it stands a chance to succeed. The more unpropitious the situation in which we demonstrate hope, the deeper that hope is. Hope is definitely not the same thing as optimism. It is not the conviction that something will turn out well, but the certainty that something makes sense, regardless of how it turns out.[3]

Is this true? Do these words express the deepest meaning of hope? Or do they contravene our common understanding of it? Don't we always hope that things will get better? Aren't we always looking for signs of hope when we wander in the dark?

There is something deep within us that responds to contrast, to the juxtaposition of contraries. We become more aware of movement against a background of stillness, and we often value the presence of someone more keenly when we have experienced his or her absence. We welcome spring with such gladness because we have just been through winter, and we appreciate the golden light of Keats' 'maturing sun' of autumn because we have just experienced something of the dazzling brightness of the summer months. The soul of music is the intermingling of sound and silence, and sometimes the purest joy follows deep sadness and sorrow. As for hope, it is never so precious as when it lifts our spirits after a time of anguish and despair. Indeed, it is when we experience lack, privation, sorrow or hardship that hope rises in us – for, as St Paul says, we don't hope for things we already possess in abundance, or for things to which we are indifferent. Especially in times of desolation, when we long for our burden to be eased, hope is our lifeline, and we gratefully grasp any signs of hope that may come our way.

The Magnificat (Luke 2:46-55), the prayer of Mary, the mother of Jesus, seems to underline the essential mystery of hope, which that quotation from Havel seeks to express: the certainty that what is hoped for makes sense to God, even when its meaning presently escapes us and all we see is failure. In her prayer, Mary unites the human and the divine, and enfolds in God's mercy the whole of creation, echoing the Psalmist: 'I trusted even when I said, I am greatly afflicted' (Psalm 116.10). Expressing deep emotion and strong conviction, Mary addresses God as the Almighty One, but she knows that God exercises power most of all in caring for the powerless, for the poor and the needy. To hope means to pass through diminishment, and Mary knows this. She knows what it means to live in hope in a broken world: she fearlessly acknowledges the injustice she sees, but she places her hope in the divine promises, which she trusts will transform the existing reality. 'Hope', wrote Henri Nouwen, 'is based on the premise that the other gives only what is good. Hope includes an openness by which you wait for the other to make his loving promise come true, even though you never know when, where or how this might happen.'⁴ It is this hope that Mary gives voice to in the Magnificat.

What does it mean to hope for God's promise to be fulfilled when we witness the desperation of poor and hungry people, the greed of those who exploit others, the violence of those who attack the weak? Mary knows that waiting in hope is not passivity. She honours God's presence in the midst of the sorrows and struggles of life, and is confident that God will fulfil his promises. Her words recall the great reversals of salvation history: poverty, not riches, is what counts with God; humility and weakness are more important than pride and strength. The divine promise is the source of her hope, a hope that is strong but also humble and vulnerable. In the midst of confusion and misery, cruelty and tragedy, that promise points to a different future when peace and love will prevail. Mary's trust in God is unwavering and she sees signs of hope everywhere: God, she sings, 'has shown strength with his arm; he has scattered the proud in the thoughts of their hearts. He has brought down the powerful from their thrones, and lifted the lowly; he has filled the hungry with good things, and sent the rich away empty' (Luke 1.51-53).

What of ourselves? The prophet Isaiah speaks God's word to the people of Israel: 'Do not fear, for I am with you, do not be afraid, for I am your God; I will strengthen you, I will help you, I will uphold you ...' (41.10). Do these words have any meaning for us today? What kind of future is possible for us, living as we do in the shadow of the coronavirus pandemic, not knowing if or when it may strike again? What can we expect, when we witness the climate emergency becoming more and more serious, when greed and injustice show no sign of disappearing any time soon? Not long ago, I read that current opinion polls from across the world indicate that an overwhelming majority of people have little or no hope for a positive future for humanity. Some even go so far as to predict the complete disintegration of human society as we know it, as well as the looming death of the planet. No future, no hope! After all, these people say, how can we ignore all the terrible things that are happening today – the rise in crime, the genocide and murder that take place in our world, the massive gap in standards of living between rich and poor people, the conflict among nations and within nations? We are destroying the environment – and so much of the damage we are inflicting on the earth is irreversible: what is there to hope for? Has not Pope Francis himself sounded the alarm in his encyclical *Laudato si'*?

All this is true, yet the Australian theologian Denis Edwards, in his book *Made from Stardust*, offers some welcome words of encouragement:

We live in a time of unparalleled crisis, but there is hope for our world, a hope based on God's action at the heart of things, a hope based, too, on the ways in which God's kingdom is already present in anticipatory and partial ways in our world: in those working for a just and peaceful world, in those who commit themselves to the work of opposing racism and sexism, in those whose love builds inclusive community, in the world-wide consciousness among ordinary people that the life-systems of the world really matter, in the lives of gardeners and farmers who love and respect the land.

Péguy, the poet of hope, has a similar message: 'Hope, says God, never tires, never fails to raise our drooping spirits as we walk the road of life. Hope transforms "old evenings", when we are worn out at the end of a hard day, into shining "young mornings", when we rise with fresh vigour to face the new day. So yes, there are signs of hope in our world, and we shall see them if, as Paul says, we open the eyes of the heart (Ephesians 1.18).

God is constantly beckoning us, and we count on his promise to be with us in all that happens to us. That is why Jesus tells us in the Sermon on the Mount, 'do not worry about your life, what you will eat or what you will drink, or about your body, what you will wear. Is not life more than food, and the body more than clothing?' (Matthew 6.25). God's promises are dynamic: they open up new possibilities for us, and they symbolize God's nearness. They point towards the future but remind us that the seeds of the future are planted in the soil of our present reality. God interacts with his people through promises, and we live in hope that those promises will be fulfilled. The divine promises always involve a reciprocal agreement, a contract, a covenant. The Hebrew scriptures make it clear that God will watch over his people; but they, for their part, must follow God's ways. In Genesis, God promises Abraham that he will have many descendants, and a country to call his own; Abraham's part of the bargain is faithfulness to God – he must not be lured away by other gods. So Abraham sets out for his new country, placing his confidence in God's promise, and for him, the future is full of hope.

The prophecy of Hosea (part of which is included in the weekday readings of Lent) provides another illustration of the importance of promises and the hope of their fulfilment. Hosea symbolizes God's faithful love, while Gomer, his wayward wife, represents the faithlessness of the people of Israel. Gomer/Israel has moved far away from the tender relationship she had enjoyed with Hosea/God in the early years of their commitment to each other. Hosea reminds her of the mutual promises they made then, and calls her to return to the love and trust they enjoyed in the past. This prophecy contains both the promise of God's blessing – that some day Israel will return to God – and the hope of the restoration of the broken relationship between God and his people. Genuine hope is rooted in waiting. It transcends any laying down of conditions, and includes both non-acceptance of the present situation and confident expectation of a better future: 'God's appearing is as sure as the dawn' (Hosea 6.3). Many things cause us to suffer, but if we place our hope in God, nothing will have the power to completely overwhelm us. As St Augustine truly said, it is good to entrust the past to God's mercy, the present to his love, and the future to his providence. What is certain is that God, as Isaiah tells us, will never forget his people: 'See, I have inscribed you on the palms of my hands' (Isaiah 49.16).

In the world of today, in the face of the widespread reluctance of so many people to commit themselves long-term to anyone or anything, our Western culture seems to have lost sight of the profound meaning of promise and of hope, its companion. Even apart from any spiritual consideration, this is a short-sighted approach. No human society can survive without promises, without shared agreements, articulated through formal and informal contracts, and without the hope that these promises will be kept. Without promises, there can be no meaningful cooperation, no lasting transactions between men and women, no treaties between countries and nations. Without hope, we would never agree to undertake new initiatives, collaborative projects, joint ventures, mutual commitments. It is through promises that we can look to the future, trace out a route we will take together, express our desire and determination to do something important together. Hope – trust that God will fulfil his promises to us in a way that will lead to true freedom – challenges us to turn to God when we lose heart and are tempted to give up in despair. When we are worried and afraid, God gives us courage. When we are grieving and carry heavy burdens, God's presence brings comfort and calm. When we lose our way, God finds us, forgives us and brings us back to his healing presence. Signs of hope help us to discern God's nearness in the midst of the troubles and obstacles that can block our vision. The ground of our hope is our knowledge that God is always faithful to his promises, walks with us in our pain, and enters our vulnerability: 'The Lord is close to the broken-hearted' (Psalm 34.18).

Promises are articulated through written or spoken words, and 'Word' is one of the most powerful Christian symbols of the nearness of God: 'The Word became flesh, he lived among us' (John 1.14). Through Jesus, God became human; as sisters and brothers of Jesus, we become 'divine', called to be living signs of God's presence in this place and in this time. The letter to the Hebrews tells us that the word of God is 'living and active, sharper than any two-edged sword' (4.12). Where God is, there is love and there is transformation: God's word is a dynamic instrument of renewal, a channel of love and hope and healing, of peace and justice. Even though we walk in the valley of darkness, we need fear no evil if we place our hope in the transforming power of the word of God to bring new life to all God's people.

FOR PERSONAL REFLECTION OR GROUP DISCUSSION

1 During the season of Lent, and especially in Holy Week, the symbol of the cross has a special significance for Christians. Is there any

way you could make the cross central to your personal observance of Lent and Good Friday this year?

2 'Hope is definitely not the same thing as optimism' (Vaclav Havel). Do you see a difference between the two?

3 Recall a moment when you perceived that 'earth's crammed with heaven' and found your sense of hope renewed and strengthened.

FURTHER SUGGESTIONS

1 Many people have heavy crosses to bear. What are some of the positive fruits of the cross as discussed in this chapter?

2 Sing, or play on CD, your favourite musical setting of the Magnificat.

3 Identify a hopeful dream that you hide deep within you. Write it down, or share it with a friend.

5

DISCERNING HOPE

'I pray that the God of our Lord Jesus Christ, the
Father of glory, may give you a spirit of wisdom
and revelation as you come to know him, so
that, with the eyes of your heart enlightened,
you may know what is the hope to which he
calls you.'

Ephesians 1.17, 18

In these words, St Paul is asking God to give the
Christians of Ephesus the gift of spiritual discernment,
the illumined inward vision that is as important for our
spiritual well-being as are our eyes and other bodily
senses for the detection and negotiation of the physical
world. Spiritual discernment, a gift that is available
to everyone, springs from an awareness of God's
providence watching over the whole of life. It helps
us to perceive with greater clarity that anything that
harms or diminishes us makes us less human, less than

God created us to be. In the prayer that Jesus taught us, we pray 'Your will be done', and discernment means just that: seeking to do God's will. Through it, we learn to distinguish between the experiences in our lives that harmonize with what God wants for us, and those that do not. Spiritual discernment – St Ignatius of Loyola calls it 'discernment of spirits' – is a gift of the Holy Spirit, and it is closely linked to hope, which leads us to tune in to the nearness of God. It invites us to seek the greater good in our lives, and it includes asking for guidance amid the difficulties and hazards and incongruous situations we all live with. It is in keeping with the tradition of Lent to look into our lives as children of God and disciples of Jesus in order to discern what God is asking of us in this place and in this time. If we do this, then, as Paul says, we will become more aware of the hope God's call holds for us.

Discernment in this spiritual sense has a double signification: it means to distinguish whether we are being moved by the good spirit, the Spirit of God, or by another spirit, whose influence is not good; and it also means to interpret what the Spirit wishes to say to us in a concrete situation. In this way, discernment enables us to distinguish between what is genuine and what is false in our lives, and to choose the path that is 'right' for us. The good Spirit within us invites us to open our eyes and to walk with God, as Psalm 23 says, all the days of our life; and this means deciding to reject what does not come from God. Nicholas Austin, SJ, calls discernment 'a simple but transformative practice' and through it, he says, 'we can shed our prejudices and limited viewpoints and take on a new perspective, God's perspective'. Learning to see our problems and heartaches from that 'divine' perspective, we will never lose hope. And where there is hope, love is not far away, for God's way of seeing things, as Pope Francis says, springs from love: 'God does not see with his eyes, God sees with his heart.'[1] Spiritual discernment will lead us to refuse to inhabit a world of discrimination, hatred and violence, and to choose instead to use our talents to the utmost, and to exercise our God-given responsibility towards all created things, so that justice and peace will flourish among us.

Of course, not all discernment is 'spiritual' in the sense we are speaking of here. In ordinary speech and practice, to discern means to distinguish between things according to their particular qualities and to find ways to remove some of the obstacles that might be preventing us from getting a clearer view of what we are looking at or thinking about. On the purely physical level, we seem to engage in it automatically, by making immediate adjustments when we want to see things more clearly: we screw up our eyes, put on our glasses or polish the lenses; we switch on a light, use a magnifying glass or change position. And although the word discernment is frequently associated with seeing, it applies equally to the other senses. In hearing, tasting, touching, in sniffing scents and odours, we also distinguish, often instinctively, between good and bad, better and worse, and act accordingly. On the intellectual level, discernment equates with a kind of practical prudence: we 'separate' ideas and concepts so that we can 'see' with greater clarity how we could or should think or act in a particular situation.

In her poem 'Alternative Values', Frieda Hughes has her own way of depicting discernment. With her artist's eye, she marvels at the owl's instinctive ability to look at things from different angles:

> The owl does not always look ahead
> with eyes on the horizontal
> Sometimes it will tilt its visual axis by
> ninety degrees

As if checking the position of an object
Against its own foothold on reality.

Hughes goes on to point to a parallel between the way the bird modifies its position in order to see things more clearly, more truly, and our own need to take time to notice things we can easily pass over, and to see them from a different standpoint:

Just as what we think we see
Is not always the truth, and we should wait
For an alternative view to be delivered
By word of mouth, the passage of time
Or by shifting our attitude, like the owl,
That knows it is all a matter of perspective.

As the poet suggests, if we are to see life and its ambiguities with greater clarity, we should question our preconceptions, open our minds to new insights and be prepared to move out of our comfort zones. To do this from the horizon of faith is to enter the territory of spiritual discernment, which is concerned with the cleansing of the inward vision to enable us, as Paul says, to see more clearly the hope to which God is calling us, and to encourage us to 'choose life' (Deuteronomy 30.19). In everyday life we are faced with numerous choices, and this kind of discernment helps us to seek and choose the 'right' path to take. Some paths lead, as Deuteronomy says in the same chapter (v. 15), to 'life and prosperity', because God's hopes and desires for us are liberating; others lead to 'death and adversity', i.e., in a direction that is ultimately dehumanizing and destructive. In one of his conferences, Nicholas King, SJ, once said that God has a vision of what we might be, and we already share that vision, so when, through discernment, we consciously seek it, we 'know' when we have found it. I value this insight, and feel it beautifully reflects the profound meaning of spiritual discernment.

Spiritual discernment is faith-centred – God is at its heart. Because of this, it is in a different realm from the rational, pragmatic discernment that we all have to engage in every day of our lives, when we look at different options, weigh up the pros and cons of a course of action, and then take what appears to us to be a sensible decision. Spiritual discernment helps us to see more clearly where God is present in our lives, and it encourages us to respond to God's call to hope. It is a process by which, guided by the

Holy Spirit, we seek the greater good, for ourselves and others, and for our world. Leading us through 'inward' awareness and understanding to take appropriate action, discernment helps us to live out our desire to walk in God's ways, to want what God wants, because what God wants is our greater good. If we believe that God accompanies us on the journey of life, we will remain hopeful even when we walk in sadness and anxiety, in restlessness or boredom or disappointment. For St Ignatius of Loyola, 'finding God in all things' is the *cantus firmus* of Christian discipleship; and we find God not only in moments of prayer and reflection but also in ordinary human experiences – in the non-religious, commonplace encounters and happenings of the everyday. As we discern what is of God and what is not, we begin to see where and how we should act.

'The Song of the Blind Man', once popular in some circles but rarely heard nowadays, illustrates what is meant by the kind of discernment that is genuinely 'spiritual'. This hymn, by Estelle White, offers a kind of imaginative contemplation on the cure of the man born blind, as recounted in John, Chapter 9. In the first verse, the man has just received his sight, and he looks at the people and things that surround him, rejoicing to see for the first time in his life many things that he had only 'sensed' before. He looks intently at everything, the grass, the trees, the boats along the shore of the lake. But it isn't long before disillusionment sets in; as men and women pass him in the streets, he sees anger, greed and hate in their eyes. To him, these people look disagreeable and unattractive, so, in the second verse, he hurries away from them 'to a quiet lonely place', where he finds a 'clear, unruffled pool'. Looking into that pool, the man sees a mirror image of himself, and it is a moment of truth: he sees the same anger and hate in his own eyes, and realizes he is no different from the people he had run away from. So he decides to go back to the town, 'to the squalor and the heat', and he mingles with the crowds there. The people are just the same as they were before, but now his spiritual eyes have been opened, and he sees faces marked by sorrow, anxiety and fear. Looking out of the eyes of these folk is the 'child' within, needing care and compassion, and, in the final verse of the song, he turns towards them in love. He does this because he knows that this is the way Jesus looks at people, for he had himself experienced that gaze of love. This man has moved from physical blindness to physical sight and from spiritual myopia to spiritual discernment.

By taking on Jesus' perspective, he has moved from despondency to hopefulness.

The pessimists of today are convinced that our human culture is in decline in this twenty-first century, and that we are living on the threshold of radical change, change for the worse. In the midst of the individualism, materialism and restlessness of our times, it might be expected that faith leaders, concerned as they are with the deepest aspirations of humanity, would help us to explore reflectively and prayerfully what is happening in our times. Sadly, institutional religion sometimes seems unwilling or unable to channel or direct the spiritual needs and hopes of people in a way that has meaning for them, with the result that many people are turning to psychologists and psychiatrists, rather than to the churches, with their questions about the meaning of life and living, and their yearnings for something better. It is probably true to say that the chief desires of most men and women, whether or not they articulate them, are not only political, material and social, but also personal and spiritual: we long for a more just and equitable society, for freedom from conflict and struggle, and for a genuine and continuing commitment to the care of the earth, our common home. But since religion touches the core of human existence, people of faith are also seeking a more 'inward' understanding of who and what we human beings really are, why we are here and how we should treat one another. If we are to recognize places of healing in our busy, alienated lives, if we are to discover how we could and should address some of the major dilemmas of our times, we need both hope and a discerning spirit.

Discernment is sometimes described as 'seeing with the heart' and 'listening with the heart'; it is akin to what St Thomas Aquinas called 'knowledge through love'. It generates in us an inner sensitivity, which helps us to distinguish between what is spiritually authentic and what is not, and to seek and accept what is of God and reject what is not. It can lead to a sudden or gradual recognition of what is and what might be. Spiritual discernment does not discount the rational but takes us beyond purely logical thought. Joseph Munitiz, SJ, describes it as 'noticing the movements felt in the heart and weighed by the mind'. It puts us in touch with the nearness of God, and includes reflection, prayer for light and guidance, and the desire to be inwardly free as we seek to live in harmony with God's loving purpose for us. Spiritual discernment fine-tunes the melody of hope so that it remains audible in our lives. With our 'inward' eyes illumined, and our ears attuned to God's voice, our decisions, and the directions we take, will reflect the hope to which God calls us.

The famous prayer of St Richard of Chichester simply and memorably expresses the desire of every discerning person: 'to see God more clearly, love God more dearly, and follow God more nearly, day by day'. If we wish to do the same, we will reflect on our life situations to see how God is active in them. As Nicholas Austin, SJ, says: 'By discernment, we are invited to notice, to glimpse, to sense how things are from within God's own heart.' When we engage in the practice of spiritual discernment, we become more aware of God's 'presence' and 'absence' in our lives. 'Consolation', according to St Ignatius, is the sense of being exposed to the 'sun' (*sol,* in Latin) of God's presence, when we feel in our hearts that what we are doing or plan to do is 'right' for us. And he also reckoned that, if we look within ourselves with honesty, we can become aware of God's 'absence', of times when we feel we are moving away from God's desires for us. This, for him, was 'desolation' – being deprived of the 'sun' of God's presence.

Discernment leads us to see that 'the darkness of God does not signify his absence but his unseen and unknowable activity'.[2] It encourages us to notice the inner movements of the soul: desolation narrows our vision, and consolation widens it, giving us hope, enabling us to look beyond our own interests and to consider the greater good. As we walk through life, we often stumble and fall by the wayside; but hope encourages us to get up again, to trust that we are not branded or condemned by our blunders and failures. The past may weigh heavily upon us, the present may be uncertain, the future opaque, but the gift of discernment frees us to go forward in faith and hope and love; it brings consolation and healing.

As we saw in the last chapter, God's solidarity in human suffering and death is symbolized by the cross of Jesus, and our Christian tradition proclaims that in the cross is our hope of salvation. Yet to the human eye, Jesus' death was a defeat, a huge disappointment to his followers and, as we know from the Emmaus story, discerning the profound meaning of the cross was at first a major problem for them. This is not surprising, given that during the Roman occupation of their country, the Jews regarded crucifixion as a shameful death, which the Romans reserved for slaves, traitors and rebels. So it has to be said that when faced with tragedy in our lives, discerning the way ahead and keeping hope alive is never easy, even for believing Christians. The following anecdote[3] makes this very clear:

> One day in the metro, a saintly Jesuit meets a grieving mother who has just lost her 20-year-old son. He tries to console this poor woman, arguing that her son was a good boy, telling her that God, who is merciful and kind, will most surely have welcomed him into paradise. Is it not comforting for her as a good Christian mother to know that her child is happy in the presence of God for all eternity? 'Think,' argues the priest, 'now your son can see God face to face, he can see God!' The boy's mother, for a moment reassured by this thought, begins to wipe away her tears. There is silence for a few seconds. Then suddenly she bursts into tears, saying: 'That's all very well, Father, but "seeing God" ... what kind of occupation is that for a young man of 20?'

Death, this woman seems to be saying, is cruel, heart-wrenching, perplexing, and she presses the priest to acknowledge that. We sense that she would have found it easier to blame God than to accept that he would countenance her son's death at such a young age. Perhaps she wanted to express her true feelings, saying to God: 'If you really are good and kind, why did you permit such a thing to happen to my son?' Clearly the woman was filled with anguish and she had no wish to hear what she deemed to be glib, pious platitudes. She was not yet able to discern any signs of hope in the death of her son. In her eyes, that death was, for her and for him, a calamity. She was in desolation, and desolation narrowed her vision. Her grief paralysed her, and as a result she was unable to confront what appeared to her to be the sheer tragedy of death and loss. In her desolation, she was incapable of discerning the profound truth that, for believers, mourning for a loved one comes with the promise of resurrection hope. God is greater than death.

The fact is, we do not understand human suffering; we may and often do question it, as this woman plainly did. But, as the Book of Job illustrates, there are no simple answers, and the words of Jesus, 'Blessed are those who mourn, for they shall be comforted' are not easily understood. Our Western society today puts itself through many contortions, verbal and non-verbal, to try to bypass the reality of death. In one of his poems, published in his *Book of Hours* in 1903, Rilke speaks of 'that little death whom we busily ignore', and more than a century later we are still trying to ignore it, perhaps even more busily. But in the last analysis, euphemisms and evasions deceive no one – they are simply a way of gilding the pill. At least the woman in the story above was able to express her true feelings about the death of her son, and it is clear that a transparently religious phrase like 'seeing God face to face' did not speak to her soul. Her son had not 'left' her, had not 'departed', had not 'disappeared' – he had died, and she was broken-hearted. She could not yet appreciate the profound truth that healing comes from entering into the pain and waiting on God. What this sorrowing mother needed was someone to wait with her, to listen to her questions, to share her distress, and to take her hand when she found herself forced to face the radical and disturbing mystery of death. Then, in time, perhaps she would be able to find consolation in those beautiful words of hope that reach out to us across the centuries: 'Those who die in grace are no further from us than God, and God is very near.' If grace is understood as God's loving presence in our human existence, then to hope that our loved ones die in that presence is a blessing beyond price. When we find the courage to look death in the face, we will discern in it God's healing presence. It is only then that our fears will fall into perspective, and we will be able to hear the words, 'Do not be afraid', and realize that they are addressed to us.

'Hope', wrote Jürgen Moltmann, in his classic study, *The Theology of Hope*,[4] 'makes us ready to bear the cross of the present. It can hold on to what is dead and hope for the unexpected.' Victor Hugo, the French novelist, poet and humanist, would no doubt have agreed with him. Though no friend to organized religion – in later life, Hugo saw himself to be on the boundaries of the Christian faith, and was widely regarded by the Catholics of his time as a heretic – he would surely have felt for the bereaved mother in that little story. In 1843, he had lost his beloved daughter Léopoldine, who at the age of 20 had drowned, along with her young husband, in a freak sailing accident on the Seine. Hugo mourned his Didine for the rest of his life, and four years after her tragic death, he wrote a four-line poem in her memory. He gave it the title, 'Written at the Foot of a Crucifix'.[5] Had Hugo's grief put him back in touch with his Christian roots? Perhaps it had, but in any event, the poem gives expression to a deep hope, to an acute awareness of the solidarity of God, who brings healing and consolation in our human anguish. God finds us, meets us, in the hurt:

You who weep, come to this God, for he weeps.
You who are suffering, come to him, for he heals.
You who tremble, come to him, for he smiles.
You who pass by, come to him, for he remains.

After reading this beautiful poem, Charles Spurgeon, a well-known nineteenth-century British Baptist preacher and a contemporary of Hugo, showed a sensitive appreciation of its content when he wrote: 'Suffering people do not seek the consolation of the Christ who is to come so much as ... that of the Christ who has already come, a man weighed down by sorrow and distress. Jesus is the one who shares our anguish, the one who can say, more legitimately than anyone else, "I am the man who has seen affliction."'

Henry Scott-Holland's famous words, originally part of a sermon, and often read at funerals, have brought comfort to countless people:

Death is nothing at all.

. . .

I have only slipped away into the next room.

. . .

Why should I be out of mind because I am out
of sight?
I am but waiting for you, for an interval,
somewhere very near,
just round the corner.

Nothing is past; nothing is lost.
One brief moment and all will be as it was before
only better,
infinitely happier, and forever we will all be one
together with Christ.
All is well.

Katherine Dyer, whose husband, William, died in
1641, expresses similar sentiments in the epitaph
she placed on his tomb 20 years after his death,
and her poem can still be seen in the village church
at Colmsworth, in Bedfordshire. The last four
lines read:

My eyes wax heavy and the day grows old
The dew falls thick, my blood grows cold.
Draw, draw the closed curtains, and make room.
My dust, my dearest dust, I come, I come.

The hope that lies at the heart of such words is not the key that reveals the profound meaning of the mystery of death, but it does point to something beyond this life. Hope includes an awareness of transcendent, far-off realities, and so we cling to it, especially when we lose our loved ones in death.

Our hope is in Jesus, 'the image of the invisible God', and in him 'all the fullness of God was pleased to dwell, and through him God was pleased to reconcile to himself all things, whether on earth or in heaven, by making peace through the blood of his cross' (Colossians 1.15, 19, 20). Those who have hope have the ability to live intensely in the here and now, and they find in God's nearness the spiritual energy to face not only the sorrows of life but also the reality of death, without being totally crushed and embittered by these experiences. Hope enables us to walk into the future without knowing precisely how things will turn out, but with confidence in

God's loving providence, no matter what happens. I have sometimes noticed that believing Christians, while not downplaying the cruel, grief-filled aspect of death, do not give themselves up to endless anguish and torment when someone they love has died. No one can escape the shadow of death, but those who have hope often find the inner strength to walk in that shadow without fear (Psalm 23.4). They do not seek or claim immortality on this earth for their loved ones who have died, but they believe and hope that the human journey will continue in a life beyond death. This thought is beautifully expressed in the words of Bede Jarrett, OP: 'life is eternal, and love is immortal; and death is only a horizon, and a horizon is nothing save the limit of our sight'. God's horizons are not limited by death. Beyond the horizon of death is eternal life.

One person who found himself able to carry hope in his heart when he was passing through the valley of the shadow of death was Jean-Dominique Bauby (known to his family and friends as Jeando), the editor of the French fashion magazine *Elle*. In 1994, at the age of 42, following a massive stroke, he suffered from the condition known as locked-in syndrome, and consequently spent the rest of his short life in hospital, confined to a wheelchair, a prisoner in his own body. His memoir, *The Diving Bell and the Butterfly*,[6] charts the triumph of the human spirit over almost total physical paralysis. Jeando experiences his body as if it were imprisoned in an iron diving bell, heavy and restricting, but his mind 'takes flight like a butterfly' (p. 13). Immobile, deaf in one ear, blind in one eye, he also loses the ability to speak. The script of his book, laboriously produced by means of a kind of 'dictation' that involved forming words by blinking his left eyelid to indicate particular letters as the alphabet was shown to him, is a testament to the vitality of the instinct of hope, which, as Alexander Pope memorably said, 'springs eternal in the human breast'. 'I have indeed begun a new life,' he writes, 'and that life is here, in this bed, that wheelchair and those corridors' (p. 137). In his enforced solitude, his imagination is enlivened, and from his diving-bell cocoon he catches passing fragments of life the way one might catch sight of a fluttering butterfly.

Jeando's book poignantly demonstrates that hope gives us the capacity to discern glimmers of light, even when we are surrounded by the most pervasive darkness. In the hospital of Berck-sur-Mer, a coastal town in northern France, his bed was so placed that he had a wide-ranging view of the sea from the window of his room. What frequently caught his eye, his one eye, was a lighthouse, and he came to cherish what he called its 'fraternal presence', seeing it as the guardian of all those who, like himself, are 'castaways on the shores of loneliness'. Each night, he watched 'its hope-filled beams sweeping the horizon' (p. 36) and was comforted. Hope includes finding new ways to endure the negative experiences of life, and it helps us to discern places of healing even in the most appalling conditions. Jeando, trapped inside his own body, gradually learns to do this. As his brief narrative, at once unsentimental, humorous and heart-rending, continues, we realize that he is becoming aware of an interior voice that could not be silenced. It is the voice of indomitable hope. Although in the text he does not make any explicit reference to God or to faith, the book ends touchingly with what comes across as a mute longing for resurrection: 'Does the cosmos contain keys for opening up my cocoon? A metro line with no terminus? We must keep looking' (p. 139).

There is no facile answer to the suffering that surrounds us; so many questions remain unanswered. Yet if we believe that God is present, journeying with us in the darkness, we will find ourselves able to live in hope, and we will be comforted as we pass through the valley of the shadow of death. Walking with God, we will be led through the darkness to a new and greater light that is beyond our understanding. Pope Francis, in the homily he gave at his Inaugural Mass in 2013, seems to reiterate Jeando's lighthouse image when he says:

> Today, amid so much darkness, we need to see the light of hope and to be men and women who bring hope to others. To protect creation, to protect every man and woman, to look upon them with tenderness and love, is to open up a horizon of hope, it is to let a shaft of light break through the heavy clouds; it is to bring the warmth of hope!

Karl Rahner, SJ, in his 'Prayer for Hope',[7] also conveys the essential spirit of Jeando's memoir, for although he uses conventional Christian theological language, his hopes and longings are similar to those that are mutely but intensely evoked in *The Diving Bell and the Butterfly*. Rahner asks God to help him to accept the reality of the cross in his life, and through hope, to discern God's solidarity with him in times of sorrow and struggle:

> I ask you for the grace to recognize the Cross of your Son in all the suffering of my life, to adore your holy and inscrutable will in it, to follow your Son on his way to the Cross as long as it may please you ... Do not let me be embittered by suffering, but mature, patient, selfless, gentle and filled with longing for the land where there is no pain and for that day when you will wipe away all tears from the eyes of those who have loved you and in sorrow have believed in your love, and in darkness have believed in your light.

Spiritual discernment helps us 'to sustain hope, to build bridges, to break down walls, to sow seeds of reconciliation'.[8] It encourages us to look at life from God's perspective, and to live in hope. But discernment and hope are not passive gifts. In my years of teaching, I once worked with a school chaplain who, during the celebration of the Eucharist, would often bring the prayers of intercession to a conclusion with the words: 'The things, good Lord, that we pray for, give us the grace to labour for.' This, I believe, is hope and discernment in practice: seeing the present reality and hoping for better things, we discern how we could move forward, and then with God's help, we do what we can to improve the situation. In other words, we need to make appropriate efforts to obtain the things we hope and pray for. St Francis of Assisi knew this, and in his famous prayer for peace he illustrates with wonderful clarity the healing that comes from discerning God's purpose and walking in God's ways. It is a perfect prayer for Lent:

Lord, make me an instrument of your peace.
Where there is hatred, let me sow love,
Where there is injury, pardon;
Where there is doubt, faith;
Where there is despair, hope;
Where there is darkness, light;
And where there is sadness, joy.
O Divine Master,
Grant that I may not so much seek
To be consoled as to console,
To be understood as to understand,
To be loved, as to love.

FOR PERSONAL REFLECTION OR GROUP DISCUSSION

1 '[W]hat we think we see is not always the truth, and we should wait for an alternative view to be delivered.' Do you think these words from Frieda Hughes's poem offer a helpful description of discernment?

2 Why do you think *The Diving Bell and the Butterfly* so rapidly became a best-seller?

3 'Suffering people do not seek the consolation of the Christ who is to come so much as ... that of the Christ who has already come, a man weighed down by sorrow and distress. Jesus is the one who shares our anguish, the one who can say, more legitimately than anyone else, "I am the man who has seen affliction."' Do these words of Charles Spurgeon reflect your experience of facing suffering, either in your own life or in the lives of people you know?

FURTHER SUGGESTIONS

1 Read the full version of Henry Scott-Holland's words: 'Death is nothing at all ...' Do you find in them an expression of Christian hope?

2 Recall an occasion in your life when you knew you really needed the gift of spiritual discernment and asked God to help you decide what to do.

3 St Richard of Chichester's famous prayer ends with a plea for the gift of discernment. You may wish to say this prayer before you sleep tonight:

Thanks be to you, our Lord Jesus Christ,
for all the benefits which you have given us,
for all the pains and insults which you have borne for us.
Most merciful Redeemer, Friend and Brother,
may we know you more clearly,
love you more dearly,
and follow you more nearly,
day by day.
Amen.

6

BRIDGES OF HOPE

'In hope we were saved. Now hope that is seen is not hope. For who hopes for what is not seen?'

Romans 8.24

Hope is the conviction that God's light shines not only in the sunlit heavens, but also in the deepest darkness; it is Newman's 'kindly Light', brightening the human horizon when, encircled by gloom and uncertainty, we find ourselves wandering in the dark. Hope encourages us to believe that, even if things appear to us to be going badly, good will come of them, for nothing can separate us from the love of God. When we become aware of this love, what I like to call 'bridges of hope' are revealed that encourage us to cross the chasm of our fears and to place our trust in things that lie beyond the limits of our sight. On the journey of faith, hope is always centred on what is to come, for there is more in store for us than anything we have already received. God seeks to bring life (St Paul calls it 'salvation') to us, to our world, to our universe. Bridges of hope are signs of God's nearness; they remind us that the goodness of God is reachable for everyone, and, if we live in a spirit of hope, new vistas will open out before us. Lent is a good time to look out for these bridges. They beckon us towards the new life of Easter.

St Paul seems to suggest, in the verse at the head of this chapter, that when we find we have few problems to face, when the living is easy, we don't need hope. This is true of bridges too: when the road before us is clear and smooth, when there are no rivers to cross and the going is easy, we don't need bridges. And the opposite is also true: we do need hope when life is difficult, and we do need bridges when the way ahead is strewn with obstacles. Paul goes on to say that hope guides us towards what we cannot yet see (v. 25). Bridges do the same: they lead us towards what is not yet clearly visible. Firmly grounded in earth or founded on rock, they give us safe passage over swift-flowing water, over deep valleys and ravines, over busy road networks and railway tracks. They may be grand edifices, reaching across vast rivers and estuaries to distant banks, or they may be humble and unobtrusive, spanning country roads and small streets. Architecturally, they may be stunningly beautiful or quite unremarkable, but regardless of their appearance or structure, they have a practical function: they facilitate our journeys by enabling us to negotiate impediments to our progress. They are a part of life that we tend to take for granted, but greatly miss when maintenance work puts them out of action. In this chapter, we shall be looking at some of the bridges of hope that help us to keep moving forward in the ups and downs of the journey of life and the journey of Lent.

In Chapter 3, we looked at Charles Péguy's poem about hope, which he calls a 'mystery'. Mysteries, though we cannot grasp them or domesticate them or compress them into an intelligible formula, are not alien to us, and at some deep place within ourselves we acknowledge them and respond to them. Indeed, all our common human experiences are mysteries: birth, growth, illness, beauty, goodness, evil, love, longing, loss, success, failure, death ... and hope is one of them. Péguy loves to repeat – and he does so with playful insistence – that even God is astonished by the mystery of hope. That we should see what is happening in our world today, and still hope for a better tomorrow – that is utterly amazing, a real mystery. Hope is a divine gift, so precious, according to the poet, that we should pass it from hand to hand, from heart to heart. When troubles threaten to overwhelm us, when we are filled with anguish or weighed down with foreboding, hope is a bridge that leads us to place our trust in God.

Part of the role of the poet is to reflect on the yearnings deep within us, to enter the mysterious world of hopes and dreams, and to disclose something of their significance. The Spanish poet, Antonio Machado, acknowledges that dreams have their place in our lives, but what he highlights even more is the act of 'waking up':

> Beyond living and dreaming
> there is something more important:
> waking up.

When we experience such an awakening, we find within ourselves the courage to keep our eyes open in the dark, and the source of that courage is hope. Hope, then, is 'like a bridge over troubled water'; it engages the soul and pours light into the darkness. It helps us to move beyond the struggle and pain of today, and to discern the potential blessings of tomorrow. Hope takes reality seriously – we can freely admit the desolation we feel, own the losses of the past, give voice to our regrets and longings – but it moves us forward by helping us to see what happens to us with new eyes. Bridges of hope can lead us to transcend the bleakness of barren deserts and face the dangers of turbulent waters. They help us to respond to a changed and changing world-scene without losing our bearings and without losing heart.

The bridges of hope we shall look at in this chapter are varied, but what they have in common could be summed up in the concept of art. Art manifests what it means to be human, and it does this in visual, audible, tangible or verbal forms for others to see and interpret. In this sense art is not simply a record of remembered paradise or a lament for its loss. Every work of art is inspired by hope: it affirms that, yes, there is evil, suffering, poverty, injustice in our world, but that is not *all* there is. Art, says Michael Mayne, 'can discover the harmony under the tangle of existence, the seeming chaos, and make visible to us the beauty of rhythm, line, shape, structure, colour, hinting at a longed-for perfection which reflects the beauty of God'.[1] Some bridges of hope are wordless – like music and the visual arts; others are spiritual – like prayer and reflection; yet others are relational – like love, friendship and family ties; or physical – like walking and dancing. Some are verbal – like poetry and story; others are simply good fun – like jokes and laughter and leisure. And surely children present us with a special bridge of hope, their freshness and energy reminding us, as the Book of Proverbs puts it, that 'there is a future, and your hope will not come to nothing'.

MUSIC

Music has a special role in the articulation of hope, for, as Nicholas Lash writes, 'in the music that we make, the truth of things … sings, celebrates, and weeps'.[2] This was borne out on Easter Sunday 2020, when the Italian tenor, Andrea Bocelli, was invited to give 'an uplifting message of love, healing and hope through music'. Following the social distancing regulations then in force in Italy, his response was a solo performance in the great cathedral of Milan – the city which, a few weeks before, had seen the beginnings of the coronavirus outbreak in Europe. It was reported, with no hint of irony, that the video of that beautiful concert immediately 'went viral' and the melody of hope was transmitted to millions of people in every part of the world.

No doubt life, any life, is a mixture of harmony and dissonance, but into that complexity, music, offering infinite variations on our human themes, is a unique bridge of hope. 'Music,' said Ravel, 'is dream crystallised in sound.' It inhabits the realm of hope; it speaks to the soul and attends to its longings. In every human culture, there is an impulse to make music, to express the inexpressible through music. When words are inadequate, when silence too is inadequate, music engages the human spirit. In poetry, in prayer, the words speak, but the 'eloquence' of music is essentially wordless, and through it the soul is reminded of its cravings for the eternal. Through hope, whoever we are, believers or unbelievers, we obey the distant music of the human soul, that non-verbal language that opens us to the possibility of being called to something beyond ourselves. Wallace Stevens, in 'The Man with the Blue Guitar', hints that music mysteriously changes reality: 'Things as they are' says the guitarist in the poem, 'Are changed upon the blue guitar.' The melody played upon the blue guitar is the melody of hope.

St Augustine, in his sermon on Psalm 32, sees music as a reaching-out of the soul towards God. There are times, he says, when words are not enough, when our hearts are bursting with feelings words cannot express, and it is then that music comes into its own. If, by impossibility, Augustine had read the description of the last concert performed in Frankfurt by the orchestra of the Jewish Kulturbund before Nazi anti-Semitic restrictions came into full force in Germany, he would surely have said: 'Yes, that's exactly what I mean!' That concert proved to be a perfect example of the power of music as the outpouring of the human soul, speaking without words, and making the melody of hope clearly audible to all those who were present in the concert hall on that day. The son of one of the instrumentalists wrote:

> The concert took off and never really came back to Earth. Something extra-musical was at work on stage, some mysterious force that every performer has encountered at one time or another. The weight of the here and now dropped away, leaving each musician free to soar to the highest reaches of imagination. From this height, the mind relinquished its hold over the human

apparatus and left the heart and soul in command. The printed notes on the scores were no longer the merest black dots on white paper but cairns on the path of a wonderful journey of discovery shared by musicians and listeners alike ... the climax came in the finale of the Tchaikovsky Fifth, when the great striding melody seemed to lead the way to a victory that not even Caesar or Napoleon could have imagined, a triumphant expression of the human spirit ...[3]

Music and song can indeed offer a bridge of hope that mysteriously links past, present and future. There is a wonderful example of this in the 1993 film, *The Shawshank Redemption*. Among the many amazing scenes in this film, for me the most memorable by far is when Andy, the main character, ingeniously finds a way to transmit a recording of an excerpt from *The Marriage of Figaro* over the PA system of the prison. The effect on the prisoners is utterly transforming: some had been snoozing or reading languidly in their cells, some injecting illicit drugs, others doing various chores under the eye of stern warders, when suddenly this music enters their grim, locked-in world. It touches them, heart and soul. As they listen, they literally come alive: they stand erect and alert, their eyes shine with hope. Andy, punished for this insubordinate act by a period of solitary confinement, later admits to his cell-mate and friend, Red, that it was hope alone that kept him going as he served his life sentence for a crime he did not commit. By sharing that music with all the other prisoners, he was wordlessly revealing to them a bridge of hope. Hope is rooted in the present, but it points to a potentially different future, a better future: tomorrow is not today. No wonder those prisoners were so deeply affected!

POETRY

Throughout human history, it seems that in every race and in every part of the world our preferred way to express in words what is deepest and most important to us has been, and remains, poetry. Poetry gives attention to things the heart knows before the mind can grasp them, and it readily lends itself to the expression of hope. Emily Dickinson, in her poem about hope, sees it as a free gift, offered to everyone, and asking for nothing in return. She does not mention God by name, but she suggests that hope has infinite qualities, 'divine' qualities: it is spiritual (it 'sings the tune without the words') and eternal (the tune 'never stops – at all').

> 'Hope' is the thing with feathers –
> That perches in the soul –
> And sings the tune without the words –
> And never stops – at all –
>
> And sweetest – in the Gale – is heard –
> And sore must be the storm –
> That could abash the little Bird
> That kept so many warm –
>
> I've heard it in the chillest land –
> And on the strangest Sea –
> Yet – never – in Extremity,
> It asked a crumb – of me.

For Emily Dickinson, hope, like a strong-willed bird, 'perches in the soul' – is there a hint that it does this whether we welcome it or not? Even if we are tempted to give in to despair or, as sometimes happens, when we find ourselves living more easily with hurt and pain than with happiness, hope continues to sing its song without words. The poet honours this little bird, which is undismayed by the gales and storms on the sea of life – indeed, it is in those very storms and gales that, she says, its song is 'sweetest'. She is grateful for the warmth it brings when she hears it singing in 'the chillest land' of desperation and misery, reminding us that even if we are deeply troubled, we can experience stirrings of consolation, moments of joy. It seems that to cross the bridge of hope is to rediscover the presence of the Spirit. Perhaps that is why Dickinson calls hope 'the thing with feathers', signifying the Holy Spirit, often represented as a dove.

STORY

I believe we are changed by every story that engages us. Good stories rub shoulders with the mystery of life, leave us with unanswered questions and encourage us into further exploration of their meaning. The Jewish tradition of midrash, seeking answers to religious questions, crafts stories to make connections between divine realities and ordinary human living, and Jesus of course did the same through his parables. I regard the following little story (its source is unknown) about the beauty of the earth and the wonder it inspires as a parable in its own right. For me, it is a bridge of hope:

If the Earth
were only a few feet in diameter,
floating a few feet above a field somewhere, people would come from everywhere
to marvel at it. People would walk around it, marvell-
ing at its big pools of water, its little pools and the water
flowing between the pools. People would marvel at the
bumps on it, and the holes in it, and they would marvel at the
very thin layer of gas surrounding it and the water suspended
in the gas. The people would marvel at all the creatures
walking around the surface of the ball, and at the creatures in
the water. The people would declare it precious because it was
the only one, and they would protect it so that it would not be
hurt. The ball would be the greatest wonder known, and
people would come to behold it, to be healed, to gain
knowledge, to know beauty and to wonder how it could
be. People would love it, and defend it with their
lives, because they would somehow know that
their lives, their own roundness, could be
nothing without it. If the Earth were
only a few feet in
diameter.

When we stand on the earth, we stand on holy ground, and when we fail to see or neglect the transcendent in our lives, we cease to be fully human. God is not mentioned by name in this short narrative, but the words, simple though they are, are chosen with great sensitivity to the message they seek to convey: a profound spiritual awareness of the respect owed to the home we humans share with the whole of creation. By showing us the globe in miniature, the storyteller quietly makes visible not only its preciousness, but also its mysterious fragility. The physical universe is seen as lovable yet vulnerable, and it calls for our compassion and protection as well as our admiration. The story challenges the reader to see with pure eyes, with a vision cleansed of triviality, to become aware of the radiance shining in creation. Through it we learn to expand our moral concern, and to see our human needs as part of a spectrum that includes plants, animals, air, water and soil. We still have far to go, but already many of us are making more conscious efforts to walk on the earth with greater sensitivity, more intensely aware of our relationship with one another and with the natural world that nurtures and sustains us. The anonymous author gently summons us not only to marvel at the beauty of the earth, but also to foster in ourselves a sense of global solidarity, to acknowledge the mystery at the heart of existence. As a bridge of hope, this story leads believers to seek what Thomas Berry calls 'a more benign mode of presence' on the earth, because God is present everywhere and within everything.

WALKING

Rhythm, the beating of the heart, is our lifeline, and the physical act of walking, moving forward by placing one foot in front of the other, in some sense echoes and affirms this rhythm. It also encourages reflection. Walking reflectively in faith, prayerful walking, can lead to a greater awareness of the transcendent, and through it, a person may discover his or her true calling. Because of this, from the earliest times, walking – not running, rushing or jogging, but moving along on foot with a kind of reverence and at a moderate pace – became a metaphor for a time of encounter with God, those privileged moments when, as St Paul says, we are 'guided by faith, not yet by sight'. A well-known hymn puts it this way: 'We walk by faith, and not by sight', and this includes those whose disabilities may make physical walking difficult or impossible. Reflective walking is akin to pilgrimage. It symbolizes humankind's search for God, for the holy, and is a powerful reminder of the importance of spiritual realities. The two disciples on the road to Emmaus discovered that walking offered them a bridge of hope in their search for meaning after the death of Jesus on the cross. While they conversed with their unrecognized companion, their hearts, they later realized, had been burning with hope ...

DANCING

'Those who wait for the Lord shall renew their strength', we read in Isaiah 40.31, 'they shall mount up with wings like eagles, they shall run and not be weary, they shall walk and not faint.' One of those people who never seems to tire is Desmond Tutu. Paul Rogat Loeb[4] witnessed the astonishing resilience of this frail elderly man, now in his nineties, who continues to touch the people he meets by his spirit of genuine hopefulness. He writes:

A few years ago, I heard Archbishop Desmond Tutu speak at a Los Angeles benefit for a South African project. He'd been fighting prostate cancer, was tired that evening and had taken a nap before his talk. But when Tutu addressed the audience, he became animated, expressing amazement that his long-oppressed country had provided the world with an unforgettable lesson in reconciliation and hope. Afterward, a few other people spoke, then a band from East LA took the stage and launched into an irresistibly rhythmic tune. People started dancing. Suddenly I noticed Tutu, boogying away in the middle of the crowd. I'd never seen a Nobel Peace Prize winner, still less one with a potentially fatal illness, move with such joy and abandonment. Tutu, I realized, knows how to have a good time. Indeed, it dawned on me that his ability to recognize and embrace life's pleasures helps him face its cruelties and disappointments, be they personal or political.

Here is 'a cheerful giver', a man of deep hope, a man who has suffered much, but also knows how to rejoice and be glad. He places his trust in the Lord, finds his strength renewed, and in turn renews the strength of those who meet him. To me, in his person, Desmond Tutu represents a bridge of hope.

PAINTING

The British artist George Frederic Watts (1817–1904) saw his paintings as allegories or symbols whose themes were universal. 'I paint ideas, not things,' he said. *Hope* is one of his best-known paintings, and in it Hope is portrayed as a young girl, surrounded by darkness and gloom. Blindfolded and clutching a broken lyre, she is seated on a globe. To many of Watts' contemporaries, the title of the painting, coupled with its melancholy atmosphere, seemed to offer an ambiguous message. Some of them told him they thought 'Despair' would be a more appropriate title! In the picture, a solitary minuscule star shines above Hope; she herself cannot see it, but she is bathed in its light. Yet though blind, she is not deaf; though bowed and crushed, she is not defeated. She has the audacity to pluck the single remaining string of that broken lyre, and we see her bending her ear to catch the faint melody of a brighter future.

SCULPTURE

During the first coronavirus lockdown in spring 2020, my favourite walk was from Poplar, where I live, to Limehouse, via the backstreets of this fascinating part of east London. Each day, with a Londoner's genuine delight in the rural origins of some parts of our city, I would relish passing through the residual farmlands of the area, now small parks or squares with a few trees and flower beds: Pennyfields, Barleycorn Way, Ropemakers' Fields – the very names of these places recalling the more innocent, far less congested fringes of London as it had been in the past. What I was making for was the Thames Path, and my aim was to see one of Antony Gormley's famous, more-than-life-size metal figures; this one, in 2013, had been placed on a 20-foot pillar on the shore just downstream of 'The Grapes' pub. On those walks, I never managed to view this statue from close up, but what I loved was to see that distant figure 'floating' on the river at high tide – apparently, the height of the mooring-post ensures that he never disappears under the water. In some indefinable way, I found the sight of that man, 'afloat' or standing tall and straight on the muddy shore, consoling, reassuring, his presence there a bridge of hope, inviting viewers like me to envisage a time when the coronavirus threat would recede from our lives like the ebbing of the tide.

More recently, another sculptor, Peter Walker, highlighted what we have come to see as the supreme importance of hope in what has been happening in our world since the coronavirus was first identified in December 2019. Wishing to honour all those who died in the pandemic, he designed an installation consisting of 5,000 steel leaves with the word 'HOPE' stamped through them. Perhaps Walker was inspired by the timeless words of Homer: 'The human race is like the generations of leaves – they fall in autumn to return in spring.' He called his artwork *The Leaves of the Tree*, and from September 2020 onwards, it toured a number of churches and cathedrals up and down the country, each time the leaves being left lying randomly on the floor in front of the high altar. He writes: 'It is hoped that the simplicity and beauty of this installation will give people the chance to pause and contemplate their own experience and also reflect on the wider situation we find ourselves in.' Another bridge of hope ...

PRAYER

We sometimes admit that we find it difficult to pray. We want to pray more, especially during Lent, and we make sincere resolutions to do so, but somehow prayer itself often seems to elude us. Perhaps it's just that we're too tired or too busy to give time to it; or perhaps, with all that's going on in our lives, we feel unworthy to enter God's presence. Subconsciously, many of us seem to nurse the idea that we can only pray if we are able to give God our undistracted, reverent and loving attention. That rules out all the

times when we're feeling down or irritated, when
our minds are caught up with all kinds of problems,
or when we feel so happy that we can't concentrate
on holy things. I recently re-read a newspaper article
about all this. It was written years ago by Ronald
Rolheiser, and he gave some helpful advice:

> If you go to pray and you are feeling bored, pray
> boredom; if you are feeling angry, pray anger; if
> you are feeling murderous, pray murder; if you
> are feeling full of fervour, and want to praise
> and thank God, pray fervour. Every thought and
> feeling is a valid entry into prayer ... That's why
> the Psalms are so apt for prayer and why the
> Church has chosen them as the basis for so much
> of its liturgical prayer. They run the whole gamut
> of feeling, from praising God with our every
> breath to wishing to bash our enemies' heads
> against a stone. They go from praise to murder,
> with everything in between.

If we take this advice and pray with no holds barred,
how do we know it was really prayer? Friedrich von
Hügel, a man who had a deep commitment to prayer,
once wrote, in a letter to his niece: 'You can know

that your prayer is genuine if, in coming away from it you find yourself humbler, sweeter, more patient.' I feel in my bones that this is true. Prayer is a bridge of hope that leads us to God, and God's nearness transforms us.

REFLECTION

Have you ever read something in a book or poem, or listened to a scripture reading in church, and suddenly, out of the blue, a word or phrase stands out for you, hits you between the eyes? If you have, then you have already experienced one of the blessings of the type of reflection known as '*lectio divina*' (sacred reading). The process starts with the slow, meditative reading of a passage from the Bible, and involves quiet listening, with mind and heart. Sometimes, as we mull over the passage, we hear a word or phrase spoken, as it were, directly to us, and this way of praying encourages us to repeat that word to ourselves over and over again, opening our 'inward' ear to catch its meaning for us personally, here and now, today. We then talk to God spontaneously about the 'message' we have received, asking for what we desire and expressing not only our gratitude but also, perhaps, our worries and concerns.

As we rest in God's presence, the words can leap into flame and we are touched by them. We see more clearly how we should act, what we should do or say in the circumstances of our own lives. In this way, the word of God becomes a bridge of hope: we take that word into our hearts and allow it to change us.

LOVE

Love is a mystery that transforms everything it touches into goodness. It is a bridge that leads us out of our self-concern and teaches us to cherish the God-given goodness and truth and beauty of others. Love has many dimensions: care and concern, faithfulness, trust, responsibility, respect, gentleness, and God is present wherever these virtues come alive in us. Sadly, we live in a world where love and loss often seem to go together, and in such times, or during a spell of illness, we become aware, as never before, of the kindness of people and the importance of the small but necessary services that they perform. Need or dependence can disclose not only our own deficiency but also – and often to a remarkable degree – the power and value of people and things in the world around us.

It was love that enabled the French poet and novelist, Victor Hugo, considered by his wife (who eventually left him) to be a consummate egoist, to transcend some of his obvious weaknesses and flaws of character. After the death of his daughter Léopoldine in 1843, mentioned in Chapter 5, Hugo wrote several poems in her memory, and in the most touching of these ('*Elle avait pris ce pli dans son âge enfantin*'), he recalls her childhood years: how she would dance into his bedroom each morning, lighting up the room like a sunbeam, calling out '*Bonjour, mon petit père*' as she entered. She would sit on his bed, take his pen, open his books, mess up his papers, leave little marks on his manuscripts, and then, laughing, suddenly fly away like a bird. Her gaze, he said, reflected the beautiful transparency of her soul. Hugo does not name his Didine in the poem; he simply refers to her as '*elle*' – 'she'. Perhaps, although he wrote the poem three years after her death, the pain of her loss was still so intense that he simply could not bear to pronounce her name or even to write it down. Whatever the reason, the absence of the name does not matter to the reader, for the short poem is filled with a father's heart-knowledge of his daughter. His love for her is a love beyond names and it carries him, atheistic freethinker though he claimed to be, into the realm of the transcendent. Love touches the deepest chords in the human heart and it encompasses all the dimensions of our experience. Through love, Hugo discovered a bridge of hope in the depths of his grief: he learned that love embraces the dead as well as the living.

LAUGHTER

Humour and hope have much in common: both speak the truth, sometimes in outrageous ways, but their message is always rooted in reality. 'Hope,' said Chesterton, 'is the power of being cheerful in circumstances we know to be desperate.' Humour enables us to see life from a fresh perspective; it leads naturally to laughter, and laughter can have a transforming effect. We are made for laughter – we feel the better for it, more relaxed, more confident, more contented, more hopeful. Laughter relieves tension and helps us to free ourselves from the burden of the unnecessary. It is another of those bridges of hope that we have been discussing in this chapter – it carries us beyond our concerns, serious though they may be, and, without erasing the present, somehow helps us to envisage a brighter future. Does God have a sense of humour? Hafiz, the Sufi poet, seems to think so: 'God has shouted, "Yes, yes, yes!" to every luminous movement.' This is a God of laughter – one couldn't imagine all that shouting going on without a good measure of hilarity. The laughter of hope may be tinged with gravity, but it is heartfelt and genuine. Holiness and laughter go hand in hand, and they carry hope with them.

Bridges, it must be said, do not make much of an appearance in the Bible – even the most reputable biblical dictionary or glossary would probably yield few if any references to them. Yet there is one passage in Genesis (28.10-19) in which a bridge (though it is called a ladder) takes centre stage, and it is a bridge of hope. Jacob's ladder is in effect a bridge linking earth and heaven, and angels ('messengers') go up and down on it. The message those angels carry is hope: God is not far away, they tell us. Rilke, in his beautiful poem about the God who lives next door, says there is a thin wall separating him from God. There is no such wall in Jacob's dream: the ladder of hope has surmounted all barriers and God's nearness is clearly revealed. Most of the bridges of hope we have looked at in this chapter – and there are many others that have not been mentioned – are not overtly 'religious' but, like Jacob's Ladder, they point beyond the horizon of our present reality. They reveal new vistas, new directions; they lead to new ways of living in the midst of personal anguish and public disasters. They remind us that a horizon is simply the limit of our vision. Our hope is that beyond the horizon, God's saving presence will bring love and peace and reconciliation to our troubled world.

FOR PERSONAL REFLECTION OR GROUP DISCUSSION

1 Do you see hope as 'a bridge leading from an old yesterday to a new tomorrow'?
2 Which of the bridges of hope mentioned in this chapter do you relate to most readily?
3 Read Rilke's poem, 'Neighbour God'. Do you share the poet's sense of 'separation' from God?

FURTHER SUGGESTIONS

1 Ask a child to share with you a joke or a funny story. Give yourself permission to laugh

unrestrainedly! – and feel hope revive in your soul.

2 Archbishop Desmond Tutu is presented in this chapter as a bridge of hope. Is there anyone else – someone in your family or neighbourhood, or perhaps a public figure – whom you would see in the same light?

3 Listen reflectively to a recording of Simon and Garfunkel's 'Bridge over Troubled Water'.

7

THE HOLY SPIRIT, SOURCE OF HOPE

'May the God of hope fill you with all joy and peace in believing, so that you may abound in hope by the power of the Holy Spirit.'

Romans 15.13

'Bad times, hard times, this is what people keep saying; but let us live well, and the times shall be good. We are the times: such as we are, such are the times.' No doubt Augustine said these words with feeling – the world as he knew it was in a state of immense flux. He lived during the period when the mighty Roman Empire, with its grandiose vision of world mastery, was crumbling: its once highly centralized political and economic power was in a state of decline, and it was failing to exercise effective control over its western provinces. By then, the traditional values on which Ancient Rome was founded – courage, frugality, moderation, as well as an underlying sense of duty ('*pietas*') towards family, country and religion – had long since disappeared in the echelons of power, replaced by no small measure of depravity and decadence. But Augustine believed that God speaks in the language of the times, and he did not lose heart; he saw the Church as the 'City of God', a spiritual city with the gospel of Jesus Christ as its foundation. He placed his hope in the goodness of God, not in this changeable world, and in *De Civitate Dei* he presented the whole drama of human history as the progressive movement of humankind towards its Creator. Augustine saw it to be the work of the Holy Spirit to build up the Church, to bring hope and consolation in the midst of all the turmoil and fear that had become so apparent in the world of his time. The wisdom and guidance of the Holy Spirit is no less needed in our changed and changing world today than it was in fifth-century Europe, and Lent is a good time to pray for that guidance and wisdom, for ourselves, for our leaders and for all believers.

The American theologian Elizabeth Johnson speaks of the Holy Spirit as 'God's indwelling nearness ... within and around the world, with all its fragility, chaos, tragedy, fertility and beauty'.[1] The phrase,

'God's indwelling nearness', chimes beautifully with the title and overall content of this book, and it also illumines the notion of the Holy Spirit as the source, the wellspring, of hope, which is the subject of the present chapter. To be aware of the nearness of God dwelling within each one of us and in the whole of creation awakens hope, which, as we have seen in earlier chapters, is forward-looking and forward-thinking. The Spirit influences the unfolding of the future by enabling us to look at reality not with passive resignation, but with an active hope. Hope helps us not to be imprisoned in the past or constrained by the present; it gives us the capacity to envisage a different future. It shapes and colours the future, disposes us towards change, and opens us, heart and soul and mind, to new possibilities. Living in hope is, I believe, simply but succinctly summed up in the words of a well-known prayer: 'O God, grant me the serenity to accept the things I cannot change, courage to change the things I can, and wisdom to know the difference.' For me, that little prayer – I have a small mounted copy of it in my room, and often ponder it – is an expression of the practical hope that Kierkegaard, the nineteenth-century Danish philosopher and theologian, called 'a passion for what is possible'.

Péguy is right to insist that hope belongs to the realm of mystery. It is not a package we can reach out for, grasp and take possession of, as of right; hope is awakened in us by the Holy Spirit. It is not found somewhere on the edges of human life; it is at the centre, and it is vital. Despair, the absence of hope, the feeling that nothing will ever improve, leads to existential anguish and emotional emptiness, and to a kind of mental or even physical paralysis. If we want to live with some degree of serenity, we must hope – that is how we are made – and it is the Spirit of God who stirs us to hope. When this happens, we come alive, for hope is dynamic; it truly is the driving force of our existence. We are not capable of building up hope, in ourselves or in others, by our own strength, nor of achieving it by our own efforts. Our vision is narrow, it needs to be opened up to the wisdom of God, and for that we have to rely on the Holy Spirit, who makes us aware of the God-given visitations of grace that are part of every human life, if we are awake and ready to receive them. The Spirit is the source of hope, the source of all new beginnings. The Spirit is the force that pulls us away from the lifeless things of the past, filling us with the desire to transform our present reality, and the courage to seek a better future. Through the energy of the Spirit of hope within us, the 'beyond' is constantly beckoning us. It urges us to step into a fuller dimension of life and living.

The energy of patience, which includes the determination not to lose heart, is perhaps the most practical form of hope, and through it, we discover within ourselves the capacity to keep going even when, day after day, what we long for does not come about. And it is when the clouds are dark and the sun doesn't shine that the Spirit offers us the energy of joy, opening our eyes to the moments of radiance that God sends to us even in the midst of our worries and concerns. Whenever and wherever care and love come alive in us, the Spirit of God is present; when we discover within ourselves feelings of tenderness and compassion for those in need, it is because the Spirit fills our hearts with the energy of kindness. When we are at odds with people and want to withdraw in angry silence, the energy of love moves us to take the first step towards mutual understanding. When someone is being treated unfairly and we refuse to look the other way, it is because the Spirit is filling our hearts with the energy of goodness. When life, personal or public, is filled with conflict and discord, the Spirit imparts the energy of peace, empowering us to pray and work for harmony and forgiveness and reconciliation. When we are sad and depressed, when we live with hurt and pain, the Spirit brings the energy of healing, reminding us that no matter what happens to us, we are held in God's loving hands. When we feel challenged by the power of others and want to retaliate aggressively, and when we fail to protect and respect the natural world as, in our heart of hearts, we know we should, the Spirit fills us with the energy of gentleness. These 'energies' or powers are fruits of the Spirit; they inspire us to live in hope, to face what happens to us with courage and confidence, and to do all we can to build a better world.

Commenting on what he calls the fruit of the Spirit, Dietrich Bonhoeffer wrote:

Fruit is always the miraculous, the created; it is never the result of willing, but always a growth. The fruit of the Spirit is a gift of God, and only He can produce it. They who bear it know as little about it as the tree knows of its fruit. They know only the power of Him on whom their life depends.[2]

That power on whom all life depends is the Holy Spirit, hovering over the chaos, moving through God's people, sustaining them, restoring them, challenging them, giving them hope, stirring them to prayer and action, calling them on to good, revealing to them the daily miracles of creation. If we allow the Spirit to come into our lives, we will not be preserved from the inevitable sorrows of life, but we will never be totally crushed and embittered by them. We will learn to live in the here and now, with its burdens and fears, personal and global, but without losing hope, because we know that God's Spirit dwells within us and in our world.

When Jesus ascended into heaven, he told his disciples that through the power of the Holy Spirit, he would always be with them, 'even to the end of time'. The Spirit comes, as St Paul says, 'to help us in our weakness', to encourage us in our failures and struggles, and to bring hope into our lives. This is especially true when, hurt or discouraged, worried or exhausted, we are not even sure how to articulate what we need: 'The Spirit helps us in our weakness; for when we do not know how to pray as we ought, that very Spirit intercedes with sighs too deep for words' (Romans 8.26). In the opening chapters of the Acts of the Apostles, Luke describes the early Church in idealistic terms. He recounts that on the day of Pentecost the whole group of believers were filled with the Holy Spirit, and, as a result, they were united, heart and soul. So far, so good ... yet not long afterwards we hear of a married couple who tried to deceive the community, and of division and bitter disputes among some of the first Christians. So it seems that to be filled with the gifts of the Spirit is not a permanent condition – we receive those gifts when we need them. Enriched by them, restored and revived by them, we find we have the hope and courage to move forward, to begin afresh.

Knowing that we belong to God, that God is near, even in a violent, destructive and unjust world, enables us to live in hope. In the midst of the chaos that surrounds us, the indwelling Spirit of God, whose presence is real, though not seen, sustains and supports us. One of the ways in which the Spirit keeps hope alive in us in difficult times is by transforming 'the terror of the night' (Psalm 91.5) – our nocturnal anguish, the chaotic world of our nightmares – and reminding us that 'at night come tears, but dawn brings joy' (Psalm 30.5). That joy, always accompanied by hope, is a sure sign of the presence of the Spirit, and it is especially when life is tough and demanding that hope is most clearly manifest. Henri Nouwen puts it this way: 'Hope means to keep living amid desperation, and to keep humming in the darkness. Hoping is knowing that there is love; it is trust in tomorrow; it is falling asleep and waking again when the sun rises ... And God will be holding you in his hands.'[3] Whenever we face the darkness, admit the pain, and pray with hope and courage, we are placing our trust in the liberating power of the Spirit of God. The voice of the Spirit of hope is gentle and sensitive, like the voice of the Suffering Servant in the prophecy of Isaiah: 'He will not cry or lift up his voice or make it known in the street; a bruised reed he will not break, and a dimly burning wick he will not quench' (42.2, 3).

The Italian writer Primo Levi, a Jewish Holocaust-survivor, discovered this spirit of gentle hopefulness in a Hungarian companion of his in Auschwitz, a man called Bandi. (Bandi was not Jewish, but had been captured by the Nazis because he was a communist sympathizer.) Levi perceived in this man an innate innocence and incorruptibility that even the brutal regime of that bleak prison camp could not extinguish. He saw that Bandi, in his unassuming way, possessed a genuine nobility of spirit that made him able to look serenely upon those who perpetrated violence, and to do so without condemnation. He had, said Levi, 'a unique talent for happiness. Oppression, humiliation, hard work, exile – all seemed to slide off him like water off a rock, without corrupting him or wounding him, indeed purifying and enhancing in him his inborn capacity for joy.'[4] It is a tender portrait, and Levi admits he had a secret desire that Bandi, should he still be alive in some corner of the world in the post-war years, would read his heartfelt appreciation of his friend's gentle, joyful presence in the camp in Auschwitz. Jewish atheist that he was, Levi may not have attributed Bandi's joy and hope to the Holy Spirit; but with his own eyes he had seen how these spiritual gifts could transform a deeply disturbing experience and make it a new creation. Bandi's joy was a gift of the Paraclete, the Comforter, and his hopeful approach to life was the work of the Spirit, the wind that blows 'where it chooses' (John 3.8). Without knowing it, this man was a source of comfort to the other inmates, for he carried a lantern of hope that shone brightly in the darkness of Auschwitz.

Among all the names and symbols attributed to the Holy Spirit, Paraclete seems to hold a special significance. From its Greek origin, the word means 'one called alongside', and in the first centuries of the Christian era, when the Church was being persecuted and Christians were daily facing tribunals and condemnation, it was often translated as 'advocate' or 'protector'. We find 'Paraclete' used in this sense in the Gospel of John; but after the persecution era, 'Comforter' was the more common translation of this word. Hence Paraclete is a multi-layered term, and according to Gerard Manley Hopkins:

> there is no one English word for it and no one Latin word. Comforter is not enough. A Paraclete is one who comforts, who cheers, who encourages, who persuades, who exhorts, who stirs up, who urges forward, who calls on ... A Paraclete is one who calls us on to good ... The Paraclete cheered the disciples, not like Christ by his example, but by his presence, his power, his breath and fire and inspiration from within; not by drawing but by driving, not by showing them what to do but by himself within them doing it.

The Paraclete, the Spirit within us, accompanies us, comforts us, but that presence may also be challenging, a voice calling us to see things differently, to do things differently, for the greater glory of God, for the good of the community and for our own good.

The Paraclete pours hope into our hearts so that we in our turn can comfort others; that is why Paul says in his Letter to the Thessalonians: 'Encourage one another and build up each other ...' (1 Thessalonians 5.11). St Francis of Assisi, in his famous Peace Prayer, showed that he took Paul's words to heart: 'Grant that I may not so much seek to be consoled as to console; to be understood as to understand; to be loved as to love.' John Henry Newman, in one of his sermons, has the same message:

Taught by our own pain, by our own sorrow, nay, by our own sin, we shall have hearts and minds exercised for every service of love towards those who need it. We shall be in our measure comforters in the image of the Almighty Paraclete, and that in all senses of the word: advocates, assistants, soothing aids. Our words and advice, our very manner, voice and look will be gentle and tranquillizing.

The Paraclete is the source of that wave of hope that can rise in us, urging us to move forward even in moments of failure and defeat, and giving us the courage to accept new and difficult roles in the service of God and neighbour. Hopefulness, an effective sign of the nearness of God, is the fruit of the indwelling of the Holy Spirit. It redresses the darkness that so often surrounds us, and opens our hearts and minds to the dream that lies at the heart of reality.

Church tradition summarizes the countless gifts of the Holy Spirit – gifts of life and healing, of hope and love and strength – in the biblical Seven, the digit that signifies limitless perfection. These gifts are divine promptings, not tangible and visible in a physical sense, but truly experienced, as can be clearly seen in Levi's tribute to his friend Bandi, as the 'touch' of God. Through these gifts, the Spirit mediates between the visible and the invisible (wisdom), between chaos and meaning (understanding), between time and eternity (right judgment), light and darkness (courage), the known and the unknown (knowledge), dependence and freedom (piety), and between materiality and mystery (awe and wonder). As the 'finger of God's right hand', the Spirit points to the meaning behind events, stirs a sudden recognition of what is and what might be, and helps us to articulate unspoken pleas and yearnings. The Spirit brings healing and hope into troubled lives. Hope, says Jonathan Sacks, 'is what empowers us to take risks, to offer commitment, to give love, to bring new life into the world, to comfort the afflicted, to lift the fallen, to begin great undertakings, to live by our ideals'.[5] The hope that the Spirit brings is based on the premise that God gives only what is good, and it is accompanied by a readiness to wait patiently for what we hope for to be brought to fulfilment. To pray in hope means that all our concrete petitions – for good weather, for security and employment, for healing, for basic necessities, for peace and reconciliation, for the homeless and the hungry – are simply our way of expressing our confidence in God's nearness, and our expectation of his providential care for us.

It is significant, I think, that in the Christian Church's liturgy, hymnody and art, images of the Spirit of God are frequently poetic: a ray of golden light, a fountain of living water, the dove, symbol of peace, the 'promise' of God, the 'finger of God's right hand'. If, as R. S. Thomas puts it, 'Poetry is that which arrives at the intellect by way of the heart', the poetic impulse has the capacity to convey in words what music expresses in melody: the song of the Spirit of hope. The Spirit is the breath of God hovering over the waters at the dawn of creation; the Spirit is '*lumen cordium*', the heart's light, and '*requies*', rest, for those who labour. Isaiah says that hope gives us wings to soar to the heavens: 'Those who wait for the Lord shall renew their strength, they shall mount up with wings like eagles, they shall run and not be weary, they shall walk and not faint' (40.31). Carried on the wings of the Spirit, we will be able to find joy, even in a world of sorrow, and hope, even when we are on the edge of despair. It is true that present sufferings can seem overwhelming at times, but the flame of hope, lit within us by the Spirit of God, is inextinguishable.

The beautiful hymn, *Veni, Sancte Spiritus*, expresses in serene poetic language the symbolic actions of the Holy Spirit: cleansing what is unclean, pouring water on what is dry and parched, healing what is wounded, tenderly loosening and re-moulding what has become hard and inflexible, softening and melting what is chilled or frozen, rectifying mistakes and errors, guiding those who go astray. In a flash of intuition, a breath of inspiration, the Spirit gifts us with the ability to see a way forward in times of darkness and perplexity, and to unite people who are at odds. The presence of the Spirit brings a heightened awareness of God's world, in all its amazing variety and complexity, and of the place in it of the human person, that mysterious mix of spirit and matter. When our world cries out in distress, as it does today, faced as we are with the climate emergency, and when we find ourselves obliged to live with the dire consequences of the coronavirus pandemic, the Spirit of hope helps us to glimpse a different future, and inspires us to work together to bring it to fulfilment. The Spirit upholds the world in a pervading love, and if we look carefully, we will see that the fruits of the Spirit are evident in so many of the people we meet: charity, joy, gentleness, patience, faithfulness, goodness, peace, hope. And hopefully the people we meet will see some of those fruits in us ...

Yet it must be said that the action of the Spirit is not always as gentle and peaceful, soothing and restful, as this list would seem to suggest. The Spirit is with us not only in the warm, comforting experience of union of hearts and minds, but also when there are misunderstandings and problems. Sometimes the outpourings of the Holy Spirit illumine and reveal, sometimes they confirm and inspire, but they can also disturb and challenge. Bishop John V. Taylor, in his classic book about the Holy Spirit and the Christian mission, said that 'The Holy Spirit is the power which opens eyes that are closed, hearts that are unaware and minds that shrink from too much reality.'[6] Francis Gerald Downing's song, based on the ninth-century hymn *Veni, Creator Spiritus*, takes the same approach. Downing's words, together with the deliberately jarring arrangement of the original plainsong melody, emphasize that the role of the Spirit can sometimes be to wake us up, to force us to confront life as it really is, and to be ready to make changes so that the way we live will be more in keeping with the example and teaching of Jesus. The hope the Spirit brings transforms the present: it brings solace and courage, but it can also upset our old ideas and urge us to take a new direction. (In some languages, including Hebrew, nouns are gendered, and since the Hebrew word for spirit/wind, '*ruach*', is feminine, the Spirit is addressed in verse 4 as 'Lady'.)

> Rage, Wisdom, and our lives inflame
> so living never rests the same:
> you are creative power and art
> to blow our mind and wrack our heart.

> As fiery gale, as storm of love,
> discomfort, burn, all wrong remove,

exposing with your searing light
the lovelessness we keep from sight.

Disrupt and right our unjust ways
with the abrasion of your grace,
while we're your foes let no rest come
till to Christ's love you've brought us home.

You gust and burn through time and space,
and strange your beauty, fierce your face.
Disturb our sleep and break our peace;
till Christ's love win, don't, Lady, cease.

Bring us to know the Father, Son,
and you with them is love as one,
that through the ages all along
this may be our endless song:

Praise to love's eternal merit,
Father, Son and Holy Spirit. Amen.

Christians believe that the Holy Spirit brings love
and hope into our lives, but this version of the hymn
makes it clear that he also brings challenge, 'exposing
with searing light the lovelessness we keep from

sight'. The Spirit brings joy – the kind of joy that bubbles out in smiles and laughter, saving us from depressive seriousness in our efforts to know the unknowable – but also a longing for true justice that makes us uneasy because we know we do not always act justly ourselves: 'Disrupt and right our unjust ways ...' The Spirit's visitations of grace come to us not only when we are actively involved in expressing our faith and doing 'good works', but also in prayer and contemplation; not only in times of unrelenting struggle to do what we know to be right, but also in moments of stillness, when we find ourselves able to hear a new or unwanted message with greater clarity: 'Disturb our sleep and break our peace ...' We ask the Spirit of wisdom to 'inflame' our lives, 'so living never rests the same'.

On the last page of his book about the Holy Spirit,[7] John V. Taylor offers a poignant example of the wordless action of the Holy Spirit in human lives, and the hope that it brings. He tells the true story of a West Indian woman whose husband had died in a street accident in London. It seems that when the police came to this woman's home to tell her what had happened, she simply could not take it in:

The shock of grief stunned her like a blow, she sank into a corner of the sofa and sat there rigid and unhearing. For a long time, her terrible tranced look continued to embarrass the family, friends and officials who came and went. Then the schoolteacher of one of her children, an Englishwoman, called and, seeing how things were, went and sat beside her. Without a word, she threw an arm round the tight shoulders, clasping them with her full strength. The white cheek was thrust hard against the brown. Then as the unrelenting pain seeped through to her the newcomer's tears began to flow, falling on their two hands linked in the woman's lap. For a long time that is all that was happening. And then at last the West Indian woman started to sob. Still not a word was spoken and after a little while the visitor got up and went, leaving her contribution to help the family meet its immediate needs.

It is the Holy Spirit, Taylor says, who 'is the force in the straining muscles of an arm, the film of sweat between pressed cheeks, the mingled wetness on the backs of clasped hands'; the Spirit's presence is, he adds, 'as close and unobtrusive as that … and as irresistibly strong'.

As we have often said in this book, it is only when we feel lack or absence or longing that hope comes into play: when we are in darkness, we hope for a glimmer of light; when we are friendless and alone, we hope for love and companionship; when we are cold, we hope for warmth. And usually we experience this hope, this longing, as fragile, and vulnerable to disappointment: it is real and undeniable, but also, like a physical touch, fleeting, transient. We may feel that touch in times of grief, like that poor woman who had to face the sudden death of her husband, or when, in the absence of felt hope, we find in ourselves the grit to go on. We may experience it in the anguish of broken relationships, in moments of unexpected attentiveness when our minds are at peace and we are open to creative insight, or in times of frustration and questioning and bewilderment. The Spirit blows where it wishes, truly comes to us, but does not linger. A surprising encounter, a flash of enlightenment, a sudden revelation of the beauty of the world, a compassionate glance, these are signs that the Spirit is with us, guiding us, leading us onward. All that is needed is our response: to allow the breath of the Spirit to transform us, to pull us out of the worry and dread of the present moment and help us to move forward in hope.

Hope does not mean always looking on the bright side, seeking a good outcome at all costs and being unprepared to envisage failure. As we have seen, it is not simply optimism, and it is not wishful thinking, nor is it a determined evasion of reality. Hope is a gift, and if we wish to receive this gift, all we have to do is to open ourselves freely to the new life the Spirit offers. John V. Taylor says, 'The Spirit is as free and unpredictable as the wind which blows where it wills. You simply ask for it; ask and wait trustfully; and let yourself come alive. Have the courage to lower the barriers, and welcome life.' Hildegard of Bingen has the same message: 'The Holy Spirit ... is radiant life, awakening and enlivening all things', giving us the inner strength to accept unavoidable suffering and to face struggles and troubles without losing our peace of soul. Hopefulness flows from an active awareness of God's nearness in the midst of pain, disappointment and hardship.

The universe as we know it is filled with deep ambiguities – in the natural world, cruelty and merciless destruction occur alongside beauty and splendour; and yet at the beating heart of the mystery of life we are sustained by the hope that God's loving presence guides and directs everything that exists. In 2001, Rowan Williams, then Archbishop of Canterbury, was present in New York on 9/11, the day of the terrorist attacks on the World Trade Center. Some years later, when asked where God was in all that happened that day, he replied: 'Where God usually is: always at the centre of things, always in the acts of generosity that people give to one another in times of crisis.' He added: 'People expect, when they ask that question of where was God – they expect sometimes an answer in terms of a God who steps in and solves it all, stops it happening, or mops it up. But the way God works seems to be in the heart of it all, and through people.' It is the Holy Spirit who inspires us to help bring God's vision to fulfilment by opening the wellsprings of compassion in us, by bringing hope in times of devastating suffering, bereavement and distress. God is not on the margins of life but at its centre. Through the Holy Spirit, God's indwelling nearness, we feel the divine solidarity when we are groping in the dark. In times of conflict or exhaustion, in those moments of pain or anxiety when we and those we love are tempted to lose heart, the Spirit of God is there with us, bringing hope and new life when we need it most.

Our God is a God who brings healing in the darkness through the gift of hope. There is good news in our world, but so often it can seem to be submerged by the bad; that is why, incessantly bombarded with scenes of injustice, harshness and cruelty, we are badly in need of regular injections of hope. Hope gives us the freedom to look realistically at life without being disheartened by what we see. We need to share stories that tell of the sheer goodness and kindness and neighbourliness called forth, for example, in so many people at the height of the coronavirus crisis, hopeful stories that tell of beauty and goodness, of selfless deeds and kind actions. In one of her meditations, Edwina Gateley, the founder of the Volunteer Missionary Movement, finds herself able to confront the pain and darkness of the human journey because she can discern God's indwelling nearness in all that happens in her life. The 'bright wings of the Dove', beating 'in gentle healing love and invitation to New Rising', call her, as they call us, to hope. Here are her words:

> Whatever happens to me in life
> I must believe that somewhere,
> in the mess or madness of it all,
> there is a sacred potential —

a possibility for wondrous redemption
in the embracing of all that is,
for in the unfolding of my journey,
in all its soaring delight
and crushing pain,
I may be sure that God is there –
always ahead, behind, below and above,
encompassing all that befalls me
in a circle of deep compassion.
And there,
above the darkness
that wraps me round
the bright wings of the Dove
hover and beat
in gentle healing love
and invitation to
New Rising.[8]

There is no mistaking the presence of the Spirit in the life of a believer. When I received the invitation to write this book, and was given the title, 'Hope and the Nearness of God', I talked about it with Fred, an elderly friend and fellow parishioner in Poplar, London, where I live. Fred beamed. 'The nearness of God,' he said at once, 'that's the Holy Spirit, and hope is one of his great gifts.' I had known Fred for some time, but by then he was housebound, and on my weekly visits he would ask me how the book was progressing. 'Remember,' he would say, 'the Holy Spirit calls us to hope, and we can't get on without him.' Many of the thoughts I've included in this chapter came from my conversations with Fred. He said that it was the energy of the Spirit that had given him the strength to go on hoping, even when he had had big problems to face in his life. Fred died in September 2020 at the age of 92. I shall never forget him, his friendship, his faith, and his deep affection for the Holy Spirit, whom he regarded as a personal friend.

FOR PERSONAL REFLECTION OR GROUP DISCUSSION

1 Recall an occasion when you experienced 'the terror of the night' (Psalm 91) followed by the joy that comes in the morning (Psalm 30).

2 Name one or two specific situations in our world today where you feel an injection of hope is sorely needed.

3 Is there any line or phrase in Edwina Gateley's meditation that touches you?

FURTHER SUGGESTIONS

1 If the CD is available, listen to Gerald Downing's hymn to the Holy Spirit, 'Rage, Wisdom'.

2 Re-read the passage about Primo Levi's friend, Bandi. Identify a difficult experience, past or present, in your own life, and ask God to bring healing to you and to all those concerned.

3 Take some time to cultivate stillness this week. Breathe in the peace that is the gift of the Spirit.

CONCLUSION

While working on the present book and preparing it for publication, I was struck, over and over again, by the appropriateness of hope as a theme for Lenten reading, for Lenten living. I readily admit that this is at least partly because, although I set to work just before the coronavirus pandemic broke upon the world, I wrote each chapter in its long shadow. What I learned from my reading and pondering over all those months is that hope has no logic: we can do nothing to merit it – it is pure gift. Hope can be surprising, it may even be considered outrageous; it is sensitive, vulnerable to disappointment, yet it is also incredibly powerful. It is true that it sometimes wavers, like a candle-flame flickering in the wind, but if we value it, we will shield it, and the flame never goes out. Amid shattered dreams and broken promises, hope opens our eyes and hearts and minds to deeper realities. Despondency narrows our vision, hope broadens it. There may be no way round suffering, but there is a way through it, and that way is hope. Pain, worry, serious problems, tragic happenings, personal or global, are not all there is. Hope dreams of a different future, opens our eyes to new possibilities. Grounded in faith, strengthened by God's indwelling nearness, hope draws the believer into a life of love. That is the reason why these three virtues are always found together, and why they are called 'theological'. To hope is to place our trust in God, knowing that our lives are held in loving hands.

With all that is happening in our world today, life, to so many of us, can seem gloomy and depressing. At times perhaps we feel as if we're walking in a dark forest and the path through it, overgrown with weeds, is barely visible. But with hope and courage, the darkness does not have the last word: the losses and sadnesses of the past, the problems and tensions of the present, and the apprehensions of the future become less overwhelming when faced in God's presence. With hope in our hearts, we find we are able to discern new shoots and saplings among the fallen trees in the forest, and we see fragile flowers growing among the weeds. The journey may be long, but as we widen our gaze and look towards a better future, we find there are bridges to smooth our progress. They are bridges of hope, and if we have the courage to cross them, we will discover uplifting signs of goodness and beauty and truth. Hope helps us to be open to all the seasons of human life, to the troughs and the high points, and to be prepared to move from an old yesterday towards a new tomorrow. When we experience deep sorrow, our faith offers comfort, for we know that God, who wipes away the tears from every cheek, will do that for us too. When desperation threatens to submerge us, the Holy Spirit revives us, rekindles our hope, and makes us newly aware of God's nearness. Then, knowing in our hearts that we are not alone, our hope overflows into the lives of those we meet, for like all the virtues, hope is infectious.

In Lent, our Christian tradition invites us to enter the wilderness in order to seek God's presence, and to pray that we will become more alert to that which is invisible. The wilderness is an archetypal place of encounter with the divine, and God's nearness can be very real in this place of apparent sterility and strange, unlooked-for beauty. Carlo Carretto (a member of the Community of the Little Brothers of Jesus) discovered this during an extended retreat he once made in the Sahara. To his own amazement, he did not find the desert a hostile environment. He rejoiced in his time there, undeterred even by the freezing cold of the desert nights: 'I shall never forget the nights under the Saharan stars,' he wrote. 'I felt as if I were wrapped around by the blanket of the friendly night ...'[1] God was very near, and for Carretto the desert was a place of hope. We do not enter deserts and wildernesses to stay there for good. We pass through, on our way to more fertile, welcoming terrain, and we trust that God will lead us through the wilderness to the joy and inner peace of Easter. It could be said that since the beginning of the pandemic and in its aftermath, we have all been forced, against our will, to face a prolonged wilderness experience. What was that like for us? Did we find anything of value there? What is certain is that when we come out of a wilderness, we may be better or worse, but we are never the same as before. As a result of the strange circumstances in which we now find ourselves obliged to live, perhaps we are being encouraged to look at ways in which we could, indeed must, live differently.

God is with us in a special way during Lent, our Christian season of prayer and fasting, and God wants to unlock the doors of the prison of depression or pessimism in which we may feel ourselves trapped. When we take time to pray, to reflect, things that had previously escaped us in the jumble of existence become more clearly visible. It is God who gives this new vision, God who unblocks our ears so that we can hear echoes of the distant melody of hope, God who touches our hearts and draws us towards what is good and beautiful. Hope, trust in the nearness of God, can set us free to walk more courageously into the unknown – it opens up our horizons. It is not a substitute for action, but it relies on God to point the way forward: 'If the Lord does not build the house, in vain do its builders labour' (Psalm 127.1). Hope inspires us to do everything we can to transform some of the more harmful aspects of our present reality, and it opens our ears to hear not only the cry of anguish, but also the cry of joy. Lent may be a testing journey of watching and waiting for signs of resurrection, but if we persevere, we will find, as Pope Francis said in *Evangelii gaudium*, that 'God does not hide himself from those who seek him with a sincere heart, even though they do so tentatively, in a vague or haphazard manner.'[2]

My aim, in all the chapters of this book, has been to present hope as the conviction that God is with us in the wilderness, in our struggles, in our pain and suffering, and in our longing for peace and justice and freedom in the world that is our home.

We know that when things are going well, we don't need hope – we only need it when we're scared, anxious or tempted to despair. Hope is a melody that transcends what we hear with our physical ears, a vision that transcends what we see with our physical eyes, a touch that transcends what we feel with our bodily hands. The melody may be faint, the vision indistinct, the touch almost imperceptible, but the breath of hope, the breath of the Spirit of God, gives us the courage to keep going, and to keep on trusting in God. To hope is to be aware of the mystery that animates all things, and to invite God to intervene in our lives. Hope is a dimension of the soul; it means being receptive to God's presence. It reminds us that the future is not yet written, that tomorrow is not today. And it also enables us to accept what cannot be changed, in spite of our best efforts, because we are confident that all that happens to us has a meaning, even when that meaning is, as Milton said, 'to us invisible or dimly seen'.

Hope includes not only accepting the reality of the darkness in the world of today, but also being ready to wait patiently for a new horizon to be revealed in the midst of the chaos. The beyond is constantly beckoning us, and hope imagines more than can be seen with our bodily eyes. It awakens us to the dreams of tomorrow and gives us a new sensitivity to the miracles that are played out in our midst. Hope doesn't mean continually racking our brains to create immediate solutions for all our problems, but denotes, rather, appealing to God, like the Psalmist: 'O God, come to our aid. O Lord, make haste to help us' (Psalm 70.1). For God can draw good from every situation, and to be without hope is to cease to really live. Hope brings new vision and fresh energy; it revives, strengthens and restores. To live in hope, to read about hope, especially (although not only) in Lent, to reflect on it, to talk about it – to God and to other people – can open up new perspectives for us as, in imitation of Jesus, we walk through the wilderness in preparation for the annual miracle of Easter.

AFTERWORD

If in God's presence you take a few moments to reflect on the journey of Lent as you experienced it this year – and Holy Saturday is a good time to do this – perhaps you will find that, in all the ups and downs of those six weeks, one or two sparkles of hope remain in your memory. Let them lift your heart, let them encourage you to move towards the joy of Easter with a spring in your step. The nearness of God brings hope, and hope has the power to transform reality. It does this gently, little by little, as Denise Levertov[1] tells us in her poem 'Beginners':

> How could we tire of hope?
> — so much is in bud.
>
> How can desire fail?
> — we have only begun
>
> to imagine justice and mercy,
> only begun to envision

how it might be
to live as siblings with beast and flower,
not as oppressors.

Surely our river
cannot already be hastening
into the sea of nonbeing?

Surely it cannot
drag, in the silt,
all that is innocent?

Not yet, not yet—
there is too much broken
that must be mended,

too much hurt we have done to each other
that cannot yet be forgiven.

We have only begun to know
the power that is in us if we would join
our solitudes in the communion of struggle.

So much is unfolding that must
complete its gesture,

so much is in bud.

The buds of hope signal the new life of Easter ...

NOTES

INTRODUCTION

1 Jonathan Sacks, *The Politics of Hope*, Jonathan Cape, 1997, p. 267.

CHAPTER 1

1 Paul Tillich, *Shaking the Foundations*, SCM Press, 1949, p. 112.

2 Dietrich Bonhoeffer, *Letters and Papers from Prison*, SCM Press, 1953, p. 55.

3 Ronald Rolheiser, *The Shattered Lantern*, Hodder & Stoughton, 1994, pp. 154, 155.

4 David Toolan, *At Home in the Cosmos*, Orbis Books, 2003, p. 205.

5 Gabriel Marcel, *Trois pièces, Le Mort de demain*, Plon, 1931, p. 161: '*Aimer un être, c'est lui dire: toi tu ne mourras pas.*'

CHAPTER 2

1 Jonathan Sacks, *Celebrating Life*, Continuum, 2000, pp. 50–1.

2 Chris Chivers, *Out of the Ashes*, CAFOD/DLT Lent Book 2005, pp. 8, 9.

3 Tom Wright, *Surprised by Hope*, SPCK 2007, p. 204.

4 Karl Rahner, *Theological Investigations III*, Baltimore, MD: Helicon Press, 1967, pp. 87–8.

CHAPTER 3

1   Jürgen Moltmann, *The Experiment Hope*, Philadelphia, PA: Fortress Press, 1975, p. 59.

2   Jürgen Moltmann, *The Theology of Hope*, SCM Press, 1967, p. 25.

3   Pope Francis, *Fratelli tutti*, CTS, 2020, §55.

4   Rowan Williams, *Resurrection: Interpreting the Easter Gospel*, revised edition: Darton, Longman and Todd, 2002, p. 42.

5   Charles Péguy, '*Le Porche du Mystère de la Deuxième Vertu*' (The Portal of the Mystery of Hope), Éditions Gallimard, 1986.

6   '*Ça c'est étonnant. Que ces pauvres enfants voient comme tout ça se passe et qu'ils croient que demain cela ira mieux* ...' ('This is truly astonishing. That these poor children should see all that is going on and still believe that tomorrow things will be better ...'). Ibid., p. 20.

7   Marilynne Robinson, *Gilead*, Farrar, Straus and Giroux, 2004, p. 81.

CHAPTER 4

1   Leonardo Boff, *Passion of Christ, Passion of the World*, Orbis Books, 1987, p. 131.

2   Elizabeth Johnson, *Creation and the Cross*, Orbis Books, 2018, p. 50.

3   Vaclav Havel, 'An Orientation of the Heart', in *A Citizen's Guide to Hope in a Time of Fear*, ed. Paul Rogat Loeb, New York: Basic Books, 2004, pp. 82, 83.

4   Henri Nouwen, *With Open Hands*, Ave Maria Press, 1972, p. 82.

CHAPTER 5

1 Pope Francis, *Fratelli Tutti*, CTS, 2020, §281.
2 Peter Sills, *Light in the Darkness*, Sacristy Press, 2020, p. 17.
3 G. de Menthière, in *Allons-nous quelque part?*, Langres: La Manufacture, 2019, p. 17 – my translation.
4 Jürgen Moltmann, *The Theology of Hope*, SCM Press, 1967, p. 31.
5 Victor Hugo, 'Écrit au bas d'un crucifix', in *Les Contemplations*, Flammarion, 1995, p. 130.
6 Jean-Dominique Bauby, *The Diving Bell and the Butterfly*, English translation, London: Fourth Estate, 1997.
7 Karl Rahner, *Everyday Faith*, Burns & Oates, 1968, p. 210.
8 Pope Francis, *Fratelli tutti*, §276.

CHAPTER 6

1 Michael Mayne, *The Enduring Melody*, Darton, Longman and Todd, 2006, p. 180.
2 Nicholas Lash, *Holiness, Speech and Silence*, Ashgate Publishing, 2004, p. 58.
3 Martin Goldsmith, *The Inextinguishable Symphony*, John Wiley and Sons Inc., 2000, p. 112.
4 Paul Rogat Loeb (ed.), *Hope in a Time of Fear*, New York: Basic Books, 2004, 2 September 2004.

CHAPTER 7

1 Elizabeth Johnson, *She Who Is*, Crossroads Publishing Company, 1992, p. 147.
2 Dietrich Bonhoeffer, *The Cost of Discipleship*, SCM Press, 1959, p. 257.

3 Henri Nouwen, *With Open Hands*, Ave Maria Press (11th printing), 1977, p. 85.

4 Primo Levi, 'A Disciple', in *Moments of Reprieve*, Abacus, 1987, p. 51.

5 Jonathan Sacks, *The Politics of Hope*, Jonathan Cape, 1997, p. 267.

6 John V. Taylor, *The Go-Between God*, SCM Press, 1975, p. 19.

7 Ibid., p. 243.

8 Edwina Gateley, *A Mystical Heart*, SCM Press, 1959, p. 257.

CONCLUSION

1 Carlo Carretto, *Letters from the Desert*, Orbis Books, 1972, p. 139.

2 Pope Francis, *Evangelii Gaudium*, §71.

AFTERWORD

1 Denise Levertov, *Selected Poems*, New Directions Publishing, 2003, p. 137.